I0438950

Prepared in cooperation with the Toledo Bend Project

Remote Sensing Survey of Chinese Tallow Tree in the Toledo Bend Reservoir Area, Louisiana and Texas

Open-File Report 2012–1215

U.S. Department of the Interior
U.S. Geological Survey

Remote Sensing Survey of Chinese Tallow Tree in the Toledo Bend Reservoir Area, Louisiana and Texas

By Elijah Ramsey III, Amina Rangoonwala, Terri Bannister, and Yukihiro Suzuoki

Prepared in cooperation with the Toledo Bend Project

Open-File Report 2012–1215

U.S. Department of the Interior
U.S. Geological Survey

U.S. Department of the Interior
SALLY JEWELL, Secretary

U.S. Geological Survey
Suzette M. Kimball, Acting Director

U.S. Geological Survey, Reston, Virginia: 2013

This and other USGS information products are available at http://store.usgs.gov/
U.S. Geological Survey
Box 25286, Denver Federal Center
Denver, CO 80225

Suggested citation:
Ramsey, Elijah III; Rangoonwala, Amina; Bannister, Terri; and Suzuoki, Yukihiro, 2013, Remote sensing survey of Chinese tallow tree in the Toledo Bend Reservoir area, Louisiana and Texas: U.S. Geological Survey Open-File Report 2012–1215, 74 p., http://pubs.usgs.gov/of/2012/1215/.

Acknowledgments

We sincerely thank Elizabeth M. Middleton, Earth Observing-1 (EO-1) Satellite Mission Scientist for the National Aeronautics and Space Administration (NASA), who collaborated with us to carry out a challenging data collection strategy. The EO-1 satellite carries the high spectral resolution Hyperion sensor and the broadband Advanced Land Imager (ALI, which is an enhanced Thematic Mapper Imager). Dr. Middleton provided the support of Stuart Frye EO-1 Chief Engineer, Stinger Ghaffarian Technologies, Inc., and Pat Cappelaere, Sensor Web Software Architect, Vightel Corporation who scheduled EO-1 Hyperion and ALI imagery collections amid dynamic limiting factors, including conflicting tasking requests, technical difficulties, and cancellation of collections due to the presence of widespread cloud cover. We would also thank Melvin Swoboda, Project Licensing Manager, Toledo Bend Project Joint Operation; Mark Howard, Geographic Information Specialist Administrator, SRA (Texas); and Carl L. Chance, Information Technology Geographic Project Supervisor, SRA (Louisiana). Gratitude is extended to Tom Zimmerman, Land and Minerals Program Manager of Sabine National Forest, and Tom Phillips, Biologist for the National Forests and Grasslands in Texas, for their help in tree identification. The research described in this report was supported in part by Toledo Bend Project (FERC-2305).

We thank National Park Service Ranger Scott Taylor at the Big Bend National Park, Texas, for his excellent piloting during our prolonged aerial surveys. We acknowledge Dr. Robert Ehrlich of Residuum Energy for his contributions to the canopy spectral analyses and Dr. Daniel Schlapher of ReSe Applications for his help in implementing the ATCOR atmospheric correction software.

We are grateful for the technical editing done by the USGS Lafayette Publishing Service Center.

Contents

Figures

Tables

Conversion Factors

Inch/Pound to SI

Multiply	By	To obtain
Length		
inch (in.)	3.94E-8	nanometer (nm)
inch (in.)	2.54	centimeter (cm)
inch (in.)	25.4	millimeter (mm)
foot (ft.)	0.3048	meter (m)
mile (mi)	1.609	kilometer (km)
yard (yd)	0.9144	meter (m)
Area		
acre	4,047	square meter (m^2)
acre	0.4047	square hectometer (hm^2)
acre	0.004047	square kilometer (km^2)
square foot (ft^2)	929.0	square centimeter (cm^2)
square foot (ft^2)	0.09290	square meter (m^2)
square inch (in^2)	6.452	square centimeter (cm^2)
section (640 acres or 1 square mile)	259.0	square hectometer (hm^2)
square mile (mi^2)	2.590	square kilometer (km^2)

Temperature in degrees Celsius (°C) may be converted to degrees Fahrenheit (°F) as follows:

°F=(1.8×°C)+32

Temperature in degrees Fahrenheit (°F) may be converted to degrees Celsius (°C) as follows:

°C=(°F-32)/1.8

Vertical coordinate information is referenced to the North American Vertical Datum of 1988 (NAVD 88).

Horizontal coordinate information is referenced to the North American Datum of 1983 (NAD 83).

Remote Sensing Survey of Chinese Tallow Tree in the Toledo Bend Reservoir Area, Louisiana and Texas

By Elijah Ramsey III,[1] Amina Rangoonwala,[2] Terri Bannister,[2] and Yukihiro Suzuoki[3]

Abstract

We applied Hyperion sensor satellite data acquired by the National Aeronautics and Space Administration's Earth Observing-1 (EO-1) satellite in conjunction with reconnaissance surveys to map the occurrences of the invasive Chinese tallow tree (*Triadica sebifera*) in the Toledo Bend Reservoir study area of northwestern Louisiana and northeastern Texas. The rationale for application of high spectral resolution EO-1 Hyperion data was based on the successful use of Hyperion data in the mapping of Chinese tallow tree in southwestern Louisiana in 2005. In contrast to the single Hyperion image used in the 2005 project, more than 20 EO-1 Hyperion and Advanced Land Imager (ALI) images of the study area were collected in 2009 and 2010 during the fall senescence when Chinese tallow tree leaves turn red. Atmospherically corrected reflectance spectra of Hyperion imagery collected at ground and aerial observation locations provided the input datasets used in the program for spectral discrimination analysis. Discrimination analysis was used to identify spectral indicator sets to best explain variance contained in the input databases. The expectation was that at least one set of Hyperion-based indicator spectra would uniquely identify occurrences of red-leaf Chinese tallow tree; however, no combination of Hyperion-based reflectance datasets produced a unique identifier.

The inability to discover a unique spectral indicator resulted primarily from relatively sparse coverage by red-leaf Chinese tallow tree within the study area (percentage of coverage was less than 5 percent per 30- by 30-meter Hyperion pixel). To enhance the performance of the spectral discrimination analysis, leaf and canopy spectra of Chinese tallow tree were added to the input datasets to guide the indicator selection. In addition, input databases were segregated by land class obtained from an ALI-based landcover classification in order to reduce the input variance and to promote spectral discrimination of red-leaf Chinese tallow tree. Although no unique spectral identifier for red-leaf Chinese tallow tree was uncovered with these enhanced methods, in some cases predicted spatial patterns throughout the Hyperion images revealed alignment with vegetation associations within each land class that was often observed to contain Chinese tallow trees. These instances were associated particularly with the addition of helicopter-based spectra to the input databases. It was attempted to extend such predictions of likely occurrences of Chinese tallow tree by mapping six of the nine Hyperion swaths and four of the nine land classes, but this attempt produced uncertain results that could not be fully evaluated for accuracy. Even though the final mapping showed promise in identifying likely Chinese tallow tree occurrences, the low percentage of occurrences hindered mapping performance and validation. Results of the mapping suggested that successful detection of Chinese tallow tree in the study area would require a spectral sensor similar to the Hyperion but with a higher ground-level spatial resolution.

Although the Hyperion-based spectral mapping did not provide the desired results, the associated field (ground and aerial) surveys did provide for a qualitative assessment of the overall Chinese tallow tree distribution within the study area. Ground and aerial surveys suggested that Chinese tallow tree occurrences were uncommon and were without an observed pattern in relation to proximity to the Toledo Bend Reservoir. Although uncommon and scattered, Chinese tallow trees and shrubs most commonly existed along forest edges, water edges, and fence lines, probably most in line with seed dispersal by birds. Chinese tallow trees were observed to be more densely dispersed within some scrublands and grasslands than were observed in pine, hardwood, and mixed forests.

[1]U.S. Geological Survey

[2]Five Rivers Services, LLC, for the U.S. Geological Survey

[3]ASci Corporation, Inc. (McLean, Virginia) for the U.S. Geological Survey

Introduction

Chinese tallow tree (*Triadica sebifera*) is a highly competitive, invasive tree that quickly takes advantage of any opportunity to become established in marsh, forested wetlands, agricultural fields, and upland forests (Ramsey and others, 2005a). Public and private lands are experiencing extensive losses of native habitats (for example, prairies, forests) and useable lands (for example, grazing, harvestable). Attempts to control Chinese tallow tree infestations are costly (The Nature Conservancy, 1998; Westbooks, 1998; U.S. Department of Agriculture, 2011), but the absolute costs have not been quantified. Based on the historical record, eradication of Chinese tallow tree or any other invasive species can never be fully successful (DeLoach and Tracy, 1997); this evidence emphasizes the need not only to map current occurrences but to also detect new occurrences and to monitor eradication efforts.

Through a progression of studies, we have demonstrated that Chinese tallow tree can be mapped during fall senescence when their red leaves contrast with the matrix of native vegetation (Ramsey and others, 2002; Ramsey and Nelson, 2005; Ramsey and others, 2005a, b). To obtain regional mapping coverage at reasonable costs, we used high spectral (242 bands in 400 to 2,500 nanometers [nm]) and moderate 30-meter (m) spatial resolution Hyperion image data acquired by the National Aeronautics and Space Administration's (NASA) Earth Observing-1 (EO-1) satellite. The challenge was to detect low-subpixel occurrences of Chinese tallow tree

with Hyperion image data at a 30-m spatial resolution. Using specialized processing of the high spectral resolution data (restricted to 400 to 1,000 nm) and ground-based datasets, we formed a spectral indicator that successfully mapped subpixel occurrences of Chinese tallow tree present at the time of the Hyperion data collection within all dominant land classes (Ramsey and others, 2005a). The indicator spectrum for red-leaf Chinese tallow tree explained 78 percent of the identified occurrences. Individual confidence limits associated with the mapping suggested that red-leaf Chinese tallow tree, when occurring at 10 percent of 30- by 30-m pixel area, was detected 68 percent of the time and, when occurring at 15 percent of total land cover, was detected 85 percent of the time (Ramsey and others, 2005b).

Successful mapping of Chinese tallow tree in southwestern Louisiana with Hyperion data indicated that senescing Chinese tallow tree could perhaps be similarly mapped in the lands surrounding the Toledo Bend Reservoir project area (farther north in Louisiana) (fig. 1). Although dominant land classes differ somewhat between the study area in southwestern Louisiana and the current study area (in northwestern Louisiana and northeastern Texas), in both areas there exist grasslands, pine forests, hardwood forests, and pine plantations. In the southwestern Louisiana Chinese tallow tree mapping, Chinese tallow tree had been successfully detected in all four of these land classes; therefore, we implemented the mapping approach that had proven successful for southwestern Louisiana to detect and map the occurrences of Chinese tallow tree in the lands surrounding the Toledo Bend Reservoir.

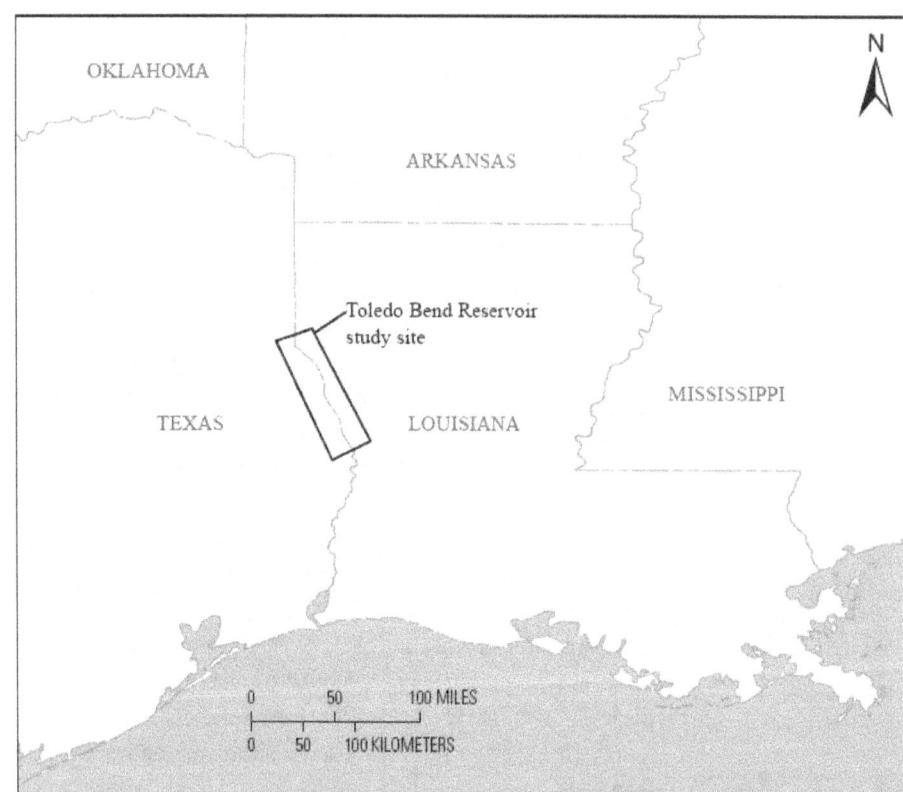

Figure 1. Toledo Bend Reservoir study area (Louisiana and Texas), as defined by the Sabine River Authority (Mark Howard, GIS Administrator, Sabine River Authority of Texas, written commun., October 2009).

Objective

The goals of this project were (1) to provide a realistic and accurate study to determine the current extent and distribution of Chinese tallow tree infestations within the Toledo Bend Reservoir project boundary and adjacent lands affected by project operations and maintenance, and (2) to determine the extent and distribution of Chinese tallow tree in the general region surrounding the Toledo Bend Reservoir project area (fig. 1).

Background

Mapping Invasive Plants with Remote Sensing Data

In all remote sensing optical mapping, the ability to consistently identify targets as represented in the image is related to the spectral contrast of the target feature within its surrounding landscape. Increasing the spectral detail of the image data promotes the ability to exploit even subtle differences in contrast so that the target can be detected within a spectrally varied landscape. Our previous mapping of Chinese tallow tree in southwestern Louisiana exploited the high spectral resolution offered by the Hyperion sensor and the stark spectral contrast between senescing Chinese tallow tree and the surrounding vegetation. The Chinese tallow tree mapping in the Toledo Bend Reservoir area also relied on the use of Hyperion data and the senescing Chinese tallow tree spectral uniqueness within this particular landscape.

Spectral Contrast with Other Land Classes

During the initial calibration of a remote sensing project dealing with detection and mapping of selected targets, the spectral contrast of the target within its surroundings is estimated. In the terrestrial environment involving plants (for example, trees, shrubs, and grasses), spectral contrast would be ascertained first at the leaf level and then at the canopy level.

Spectral Characteristics of Leaves

The spectral properties of individual leaves are first inspected because leaves are the dominant control of canopy reflectance as imaged by an optical remote-sensing system (fig. 2). If contrast does not exist at the leaf level between the target plant and the other plants immediately around it, detection of the target plant is unlikely unless other factors (for example, canopy structure or background) promote differentiation of the target plant from all other spatially co-occurring plant species. If spectral contrast can be assured, the next step is to estimate limitations for detecting the target plant at the canopy level.

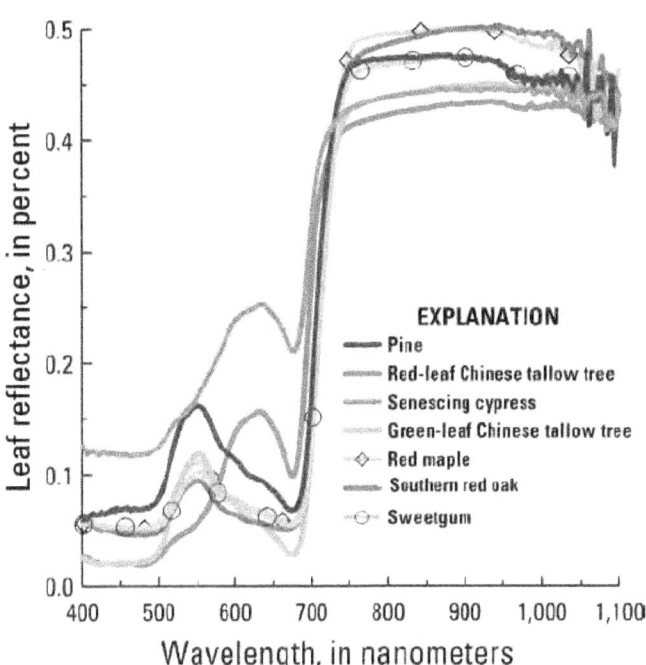

Figure 2. Reflectance spectra of leaves belonging to various tree species imaged during fall senescence in the Toledo Bend Reservoir (Louisiana and Texas) study area. Tree varieties include pine (*Pinus* L. spp.), Chinese tallow tree (*Triadica sebifera*), cypress (*Cupressus* L. spp.), red maple (*Acer rubrum*), southern red oak (*Quercus falcata* Michx.), and sweetgum (*Liquidambar styraciflua*). The reflectance spectra were derived from laboratory spectral recordings described in Ramsey and others (2005). A minimum of three reflectance spectra from each of three leaves per tree variety were used in the calculation of mean leaf reflectance per tree variety.

Canopy Reflectance Spectra

Canopy reflectance comprises all compositions within the instantaneous field of view (IFOV) or image pixel. In terrestrial environments, these compositions include the plants and the soil background. In canopies where the plants form full or nearly full cover (little sunlight reaches the soil surface), the background contributes little to the canopy reflectance. Excluding the background contribution, the canopy reflectance is related to the position and percent occurrence of each plant type within the IFOV. If the plant occurs in the subcanopy, its contribution to the canopy reflectance will be diminished by an amount related to the sunlight reduction from the canopy overstory (the amount of plant material between the subcanopy and the top of canopy [TOC]) to the subcanopy plants. In most cases, plants in the subcanopy are not detectable by optical sensors. If a plant reaches the TOC, the plant contribution (to the canopy reflectance) will depend on what proportion of the IFOV (for example the 30- by 30-m Hyperion pixel) the plant (or multiple plants of the same type) makes up the pixel composition. In most circumstances, the ability to detect a plant having spectrally contrasting leaves depends on the proportion (percent occurrence) of that plant observable at the TOC within the IFOV (fig. 3). This detection limit is normally estimated by field calibrations.

Spatial and Spectral Resolutions of Spatially Infrequent and Small Targets

There is a tradeoff between the size of the IFOV and the overall sensor coverage. Sensors with higher spatial resolutions (and smaller IFOVs) typically image (capture spectral data) less extensive ground areas. For instance, a sensor with a 1-m IFOV would image a smaller area than a sensor with a 30-m IFOV. Coverage differences have implications for monitoring and detection. The more spatially extensive the coverage, the higher potential for more frequent image collections. A higher collection frequency increases the possibility of collecting images when and where needed. In situations where collection timing is critical (for example, during fall senescence), higher frequency collection increases the chance for acquiring appropriately timed images. Thus,

sensors with coarser IFOVs or larger pixels are beneficial in monitoring and detection mapping because they allow for enhanced collection frequency and regional mapping; however, the spatial resolution may not allow detection of spatially infrequent and small target occurrences.

High Spectral Resolution Offset of Coarse Spatial Resolution

One method used to provide subpixel detection (of targets smaller than the IFOV; see fig. 4) is to increase the spectral resolution. Most resource-mapping sensors operate with a limited number (8 to 15) of spectral bands (for example, color-infrared [CIR] photography relies on three spectral bands). In contrast, sensors with high spectral resolution (operating with tens to hundreds of spectral bands) can provide subpixel detection of targets exhibiting a spectral contrast within a landscape.

In a joint project of the U.S. Geological Survey (USGS) and NASA in southwestern Louisiana, TOC Chinese tallow trees were detected at subpixel occurrences within the 30-m IFOV of the EO-1 Hyperion sensor (Ramsey and others, 2005b). The Chinese tallow tree was detected successfully in bottomland hardwood, pine and cypress-tupelo forests, pine plantations, grassland fields, and topographic high spots in palustrine to estuarine marshes. Field validations of the Hyperion data indicated that Chinese tallow tree occurrences (per pixel) were detected correctly 78 percent of the time (fig. 5).

Creation of Accurate Reflectance Images from Raw Hyperion Data

Estimate of the Detection Limit for Percent Occurrence

The degree of accuracy and precision required in the reflectance images to be derived from Hyperion data was discovered by comparing helicopter-based canopy reflectance spectra obtained from two pine stands of similar structure, one with a 17 percent occurrence of Chinese tallow trees within the area covered and one without any Chinese tallow trees (fig. 6). The nearly coincident spectra attested to the high similarity of the stand structures (maturity, cover, background) wherein the small magnitude of deviation in the red wavelength region (600 to 700 nm) represented the presence of red-leaf Chinese tallow trees. The necessary accuracy of the canopy reflectance to detect the minor distinction between the two spectra (and thus to detect Chinese tallow tree occurrences) was calculated to be plus or minus 1 percent in the visible wavelengths (400 to 700 nm) and plus or minus 5 percent in the near-infrared wavelengths (here subset at 700 to 940 nm). Based on Hyperion reflectance images produced at these high

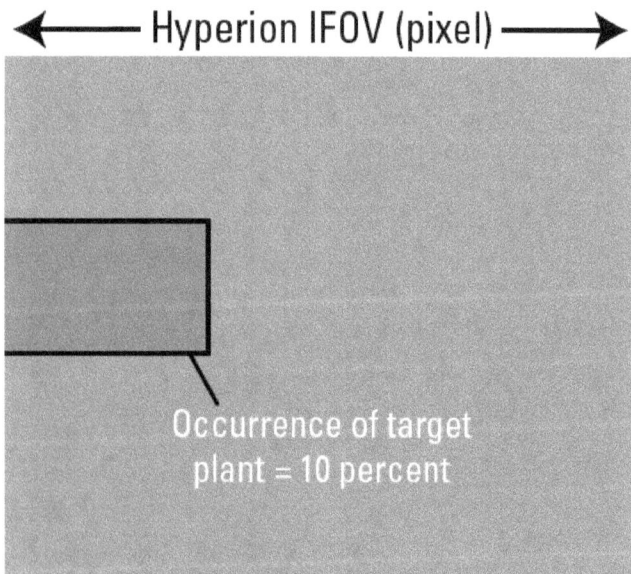

◄────── Hyperion IFOV (pixel) ──────►

Occurrence of target
plant = 10 percent

Figure 3.   An idealized representation of a mixed pixel composition The box represents an image pixel defined by the instantaneous field of view (IFOV) of the Earth Observing-1 Hyperion sensor. The green color represents the typical top-of-canopy (TOC) plant composition for the region, and the smaller red box represents the occurrence of the target plant having spectrally contrasting leaves reaching the TOC. The percent occurrence of the target plant is the ratio of the red box area to the IFOV.

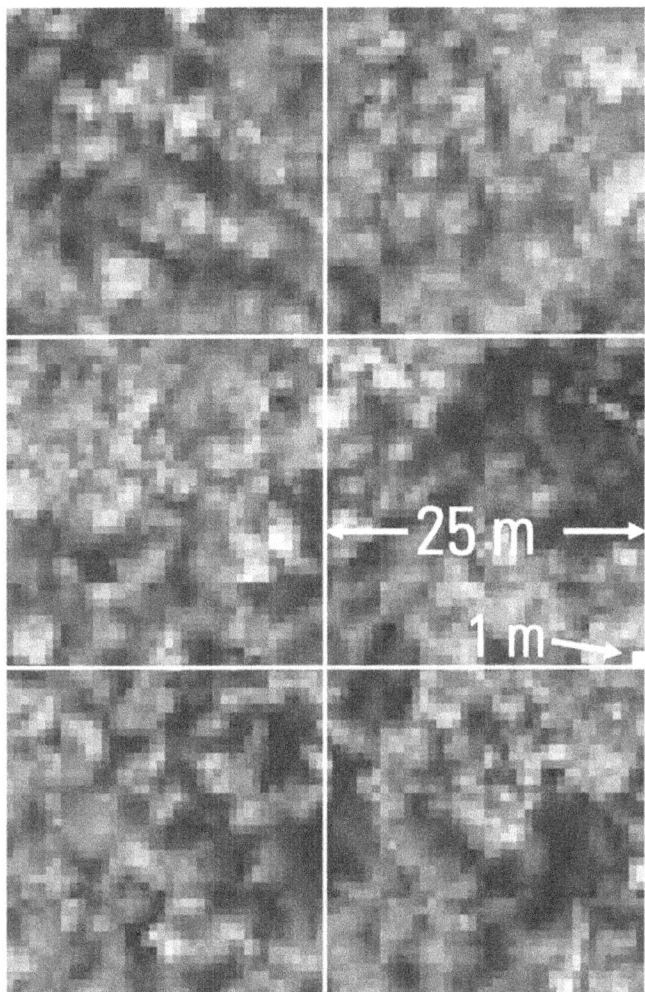

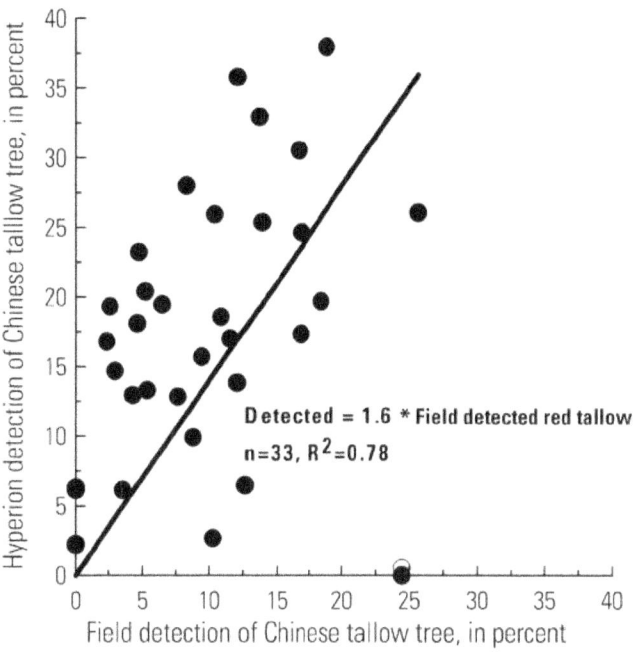

Figure 5. Correspondence (by percent occurrence in the pixel) between field-observed and Hyperion-detected Chinese tallow trees (*Triadica sebifera*) occurring in the top of canopy at 34 field sites (Ramsey and others, 2005b). The field sites included all major land classes within the imaged area.

Figure 4. Color-infrared (CIR) photographs of a mixed hardwood and pine forest in southwestern Louisiana during fall senescence (Ramsey and others, 2002). Green foliage of hardwoods is depicted in red, and red foliage of Chinese tallow tree (*Triadica sebifera*), with a fairly high percent occurrence, is depicted in yellow. The instantaneous field of view (IFOV) of the CIR photography is 1 meter (m). The overlain grid simulates a sensor with an IFOV of 25 m (or a 25-m pixel). Although the 1-m CIR photography accurately detected the top-of-canopy positioned red-leaf Chinese tallow trees, it comprised only a portion of the 25-m pixel (subpixel cover).

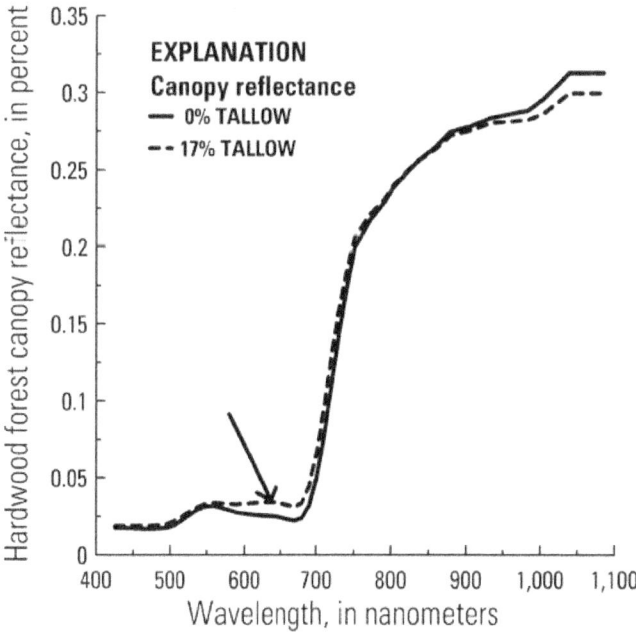

Figure 6. Reflectance spectra of two pine (*Pinus* L. spp) stands, one with and one without Chinese tallow trees (*Triadica sebifera*). The spectra were obtained by following methods described in Ramsey and others (2005b). Note the difference in spectral magnitude in the red wavelengths (600 to 700 nanometers [nm]) when Chinese tallow trees were present.

accuracies, red-leaf Chinese tallow trees were estimated to be detected 68 percent of the time when occupying 10 percent of the TOC area (or 30- by 30-m pixel) and 85 percent of the time when occupying 15 percent of the TOC area (Ramsey and others, 2005b).

Derivation of Canopy Reflectance Image from Hyperion Data

To achieve an acceptable level of precision and accuracy in the canopy reflectance values derived from raw Hyperion data, we used an atmospheric correction radiative transfer model driven by a nonlinear optimization procedure (Ramsey and Nelson, 2005) (fig. 7). The objective of the model was to transform the raw Hyperion spectra to reflectance spectra representing the intrinsic properties of the canopy composition. Results of the atmospheric correction and the subsequent normalization of the raw Hyperion data provided estimates of canopy reflectance with a 1 percent maximum reflectance error in the visible wavelengths and a 5 percent maximum reflectance error in the near-infrared wavelengths (fig. 8).

Creation of the Indicator Spectrum for Chinese Tallow Tree

Creation of an indicator spectrum for Chinese tallow tree, along with indicator spectra for all other dominant land classes, was accomplished by using the spectral analysis program suite, PolyVector Analysis (PVA) (Ramsey and others, 2005a). The objective of a PVA program is to identify those component spectra that can be linearly combined to reproduce all spectra within the input set, in this case, the Hyperion reflectance image. Although the physical process differs, separation of visible sunlight into its blue, green, and red components illustrates the similar objective of PVA (fig. 9). PVA identifies the minimum and unique set of indicator spectra that will reconstruct the spectral variance of the input dataset. Once those unique spectra are defined, they can be used to calculate the proportion of each identified spectra in each unknown composite (for example, sunlight illumination spectra). In this study, each pixel in a Hyperion image defines an input composite spectrum. As in a previous study on detecting Chinese tallow tree in southwestern Louisiana (Ramsey and others, 2005a, b), the three component spectra— red-leaf (senescing) Chinese tallow tree, green vegetation, and senescent vegetation (other than Chinese tallow tree)— identified by PVA were used to determine the relative percent occurrences of each component in each Hyperion pixel (fig. 10). Three maps, one representing the percent occurrence of red-leaf Chinese tallow tree, one representing green vegetation, and one representing senescent vegetation were produced (Ramsey and others, 2005a).

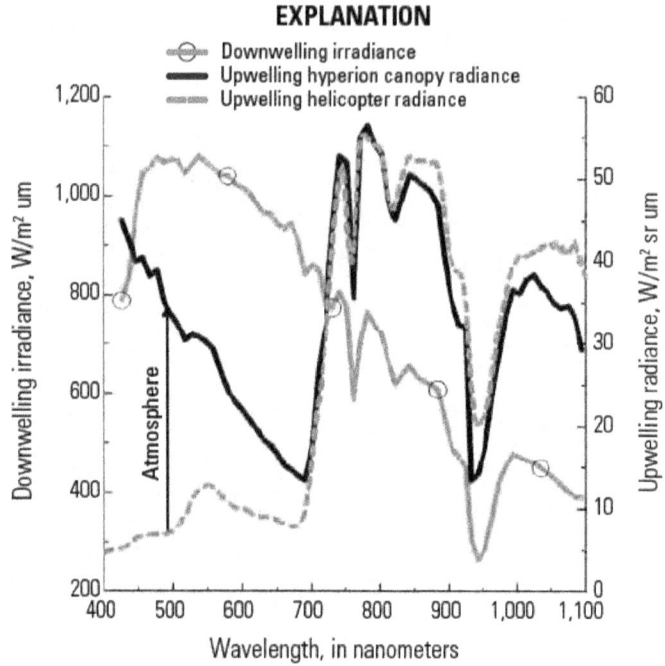

Figure 7. Downwelling sunlight (irradiance) illuminating the forest canopy, upwelling spectra obtained from a raw Hyperion image, and canopy reflectance (used for calibration in the atmospheric correction of the Hyperion image data) obtained from a helicopter platform with a handheld radiometer. The ground-based downwelling irradiance and the helicopter-based upwelling recordings were done simultaneously.

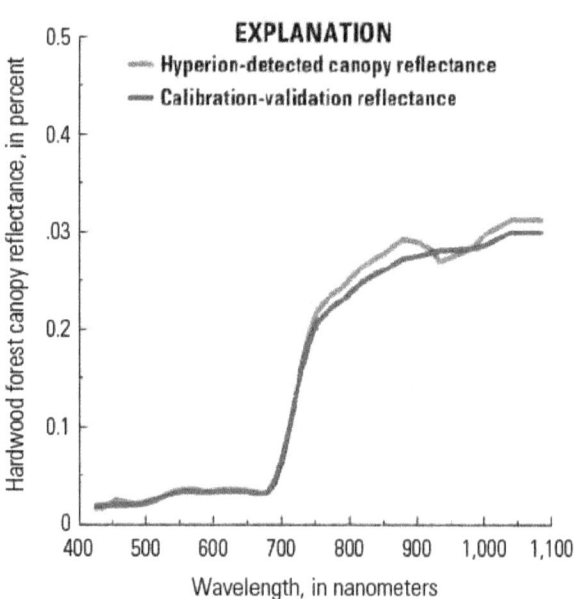

Figure 8. A canopy reflectance spectrum obtained with a handheld radiometer from a helicopter platform and a canopy reflectance spectrum derived from a raw Hyperion image by using the simultaneous downwelling sunlight recordings (fig. 7) and an atmospheric correction model. Correspondence between the helicopter-based calibration-validation and the atmospherically corrected and normalized Hyperion reflectance spectra is extremely close.

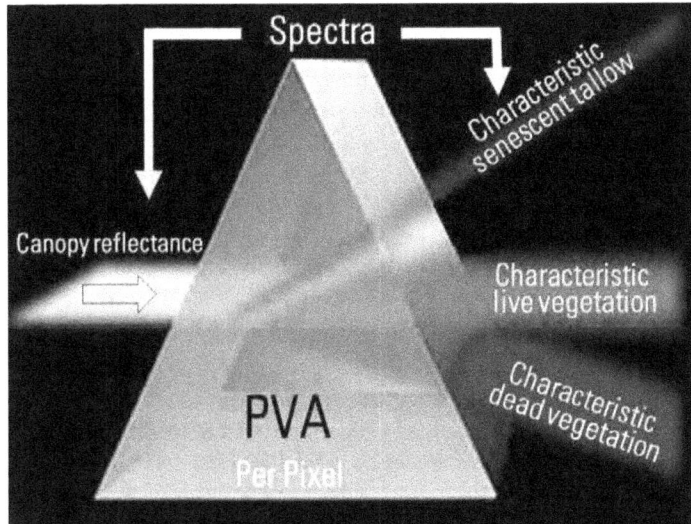

Figure 9.   The characteristic components (indicator spectra) of the composite spectrum of visible sunlight wherein the characteristic component spectra are the blue, green, and red wavelengths in each Hyperion pixel. The prism represents the spectral separator mechanism of the PolyVector Analysis (PVA), and the indicator spectra represent the senescent tallow, that is, red-leaf Chinese tallow trees (*Triadica sebifera*), along with live (green) and dead (senescent) vegetation that comprise the canopy within the pixel coverage.

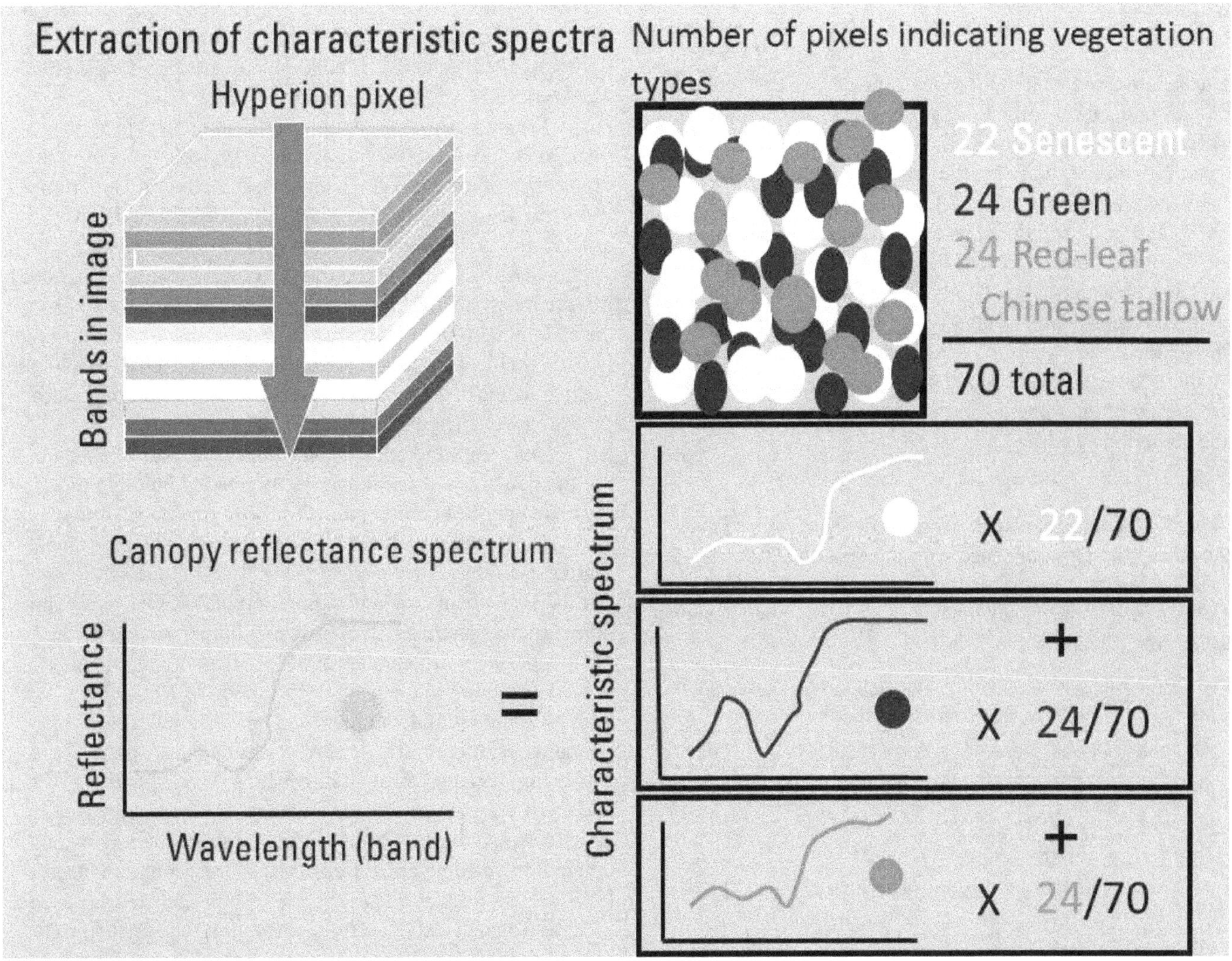

Extraction of characteristic spectra

Hyperion pixel

Bands in image

Canopy reflectance spectrum

Reflectance

Wavelength (band)

Number of pixels indicating vegetation types

22 Senescent

24 Green

24 Red-leaf Chinese tallow

70 total

Characteristic spectrum

=

X 22/70

+

X 24/70

+

X 24/70

Figure 10.   An illustration of how the linear addition of each component or indicator spectrum (red, blue, and yellow) that best reproduces the composite spectrum (green) of the Hyperion pixel. The indicator spectra are related to the percent occurrence of each vegetation class represented in the pixel by using ground observations of canopy compositions and helicopter-based calibration spectra. In this case, the combination of indicator spectra (spectral components) for the red-leaf Chinese tallow tree (*Triadica sebifera*), green (live) vegetation, and senescent vegetation define the proportions of each land class in the target pixel.

Methods

The Strategy for Collecting Hyperion Imagery of the Toledo Bend Reservoir Area

The narrow 7.7-kilometer (km) east-to-west width of the Hyperion image swath required the formulation of a collection strategy (fig. 11) to accommodate the necessary coverage of the Louisiana and Texas sides of the Toledo Bend Reservoir (wider than a single-swath coverage) and to obtain the priority coverages requested by the Toledo Bend Authority.

Simultaneously Collecting Hyperion and Advanced Land Imager Data

The Hyperion image data were transferred by NASA to the USGS as * hrd and *.L1R files. The data contained 242 image bands wherein each represented a specific wavelength. The Hyperion files were downloaded from a NASA Web site, reformatted, and input to the atmospheric correction and normalization software. The simultaneously collected Advanced Land Imager (ALI) data were downloaded from the same NASA site. ALI data files contained nine multispectral bands of which six replicated Landsat Thematic Mapper bands and three additional bands to enhance the mapping performance of the ALI sensor (table 1) (the ALI sensor also includes a panchromatic band). The 7.7-km wide swath of the Hyperion sensor was located on the most western portion of the 37-km wide swath of the ALI image (fig. 12). The more spatially extensive ALI swath produced a higher imaging frequency of the same location within the project area than did the Hyperion swath.

Table 1.   Spectral band centers of imagery acquired by the Advanced Land Imager sensor onboard the Earth Observing-1 satellite. Imagery was used for mapping occurrences of Chinese tallow trees (*Triadica sebifera*) within the Toledo Bend Reservoir study area (Louisiana and Texas).

[ALI, Advanced Land Imager; TM, thematic mapper; nm, nanometers; IFOV, instantaneous field of view; m, meter; MS, multispectral]

ALI band	Landsat TM band	Wavelength (nm)	IFOV (m)
Pan		480–690	10 x 10
1	MS-1'	433–453	30 x 30
2	MS - 1	450–515	30 x 30
3	MS - 2	525–605	30 x 30
4	MS - 3	630–690	30 x 30
5	MS - 4	775–805	30 x 30
6	MS - 4'	845–890	30 x 30
7	MS - 5'	1,200–1,300	30 x 30
8	MS - 5	1,550–1,750	30 x 30
9	MS - 7	2,080–2,350	30 x 30

Creating Hyperion Reflectance Images

The transformation of the raw Hyperion data into canopy-reflectance estimates was to follow a previously developed successful strategy (Ramsey and Nelson, 2005). That strategy used the combined canopy-reflectance validation data derived from targeted helicopter-based upwelling and ground-based downwelling light measurements for validation of Hyperion spectra adjusted by using an atmospheric correction model. The result of this procedure was the transformation of raw Hyperion image data to reflectance estimates (for example, figs. 7 and 8). In this study, however, stabilization difficulties and timing issues during the helicopter survey resulted in only a limited number of validation-reflectance spectra being produced. That limited set of validation-reflectance spectra was inadequate for reproducing the previous transformation of Hyperion data based on Ramsey and Nelson (2005). In order to derive canopy-reflectance estimates from the raw Hyperion data, we purchased and applied (with adjustments, alterations, and adaptions) the proprietary atmospheric correction program, Atmospheric /Topographic Correction for Satellite Imagery (ATCOR) (Richter and Schläpfer, 2011).

The first step in producing Hyperion reflectance images was to choose an appropriate range of wavelengths from the full range of the available bands. Degradation of Hyperion spectral bands from 2002 to 2009 necessitated revision of spectral templates used in our previously developed atmospheric-correction programs (Ramsey and Nelson, 2005). In the initial inspections, the short-wavelength bandwidths used in 2003 (400 to 450 nm) were not useable. After testing, the workable wavelength range extended from 450 to 920 nm, which includes most of the visible and about half of the near-infrared wavelengths (table 2).

Next, the suite of ATCOR programs had to be adapted to the new wavelength ranges. This entailed building new wavelength files compatible with the source-code structure of ATCOR and implementing these via specialty programs into the database files used by ATCOR. Also during the initial implementation and calibration of ATCOR, user-input operational parameters that provided initial starting points were chosen by trial and error via application iterations.

In addition to tailoring the initiation of ATCOR via reformation of data inputs and optimization of user parameters, more intricate corrections and alterations were implemented through direct consultations with ATCOR program creators. A number of refinements were implemented to the ATCOR code, and subsequent revisions were implemented and tested. These corrections enhanced ATCOR performance specific to the Hyperion datasets used for the Toledo Bend Reservoir study area. The final ATCOR-based canopy-reflectance estimates from the raw Hyperion data were greatly improved beyond the products created by the initial (nonrevised) ATCOR software version. Within that improvement process, we found that the Hyperion sensor had degraded and inherent signal noise of the sensor seemed increased since we previously conducted a Chinese

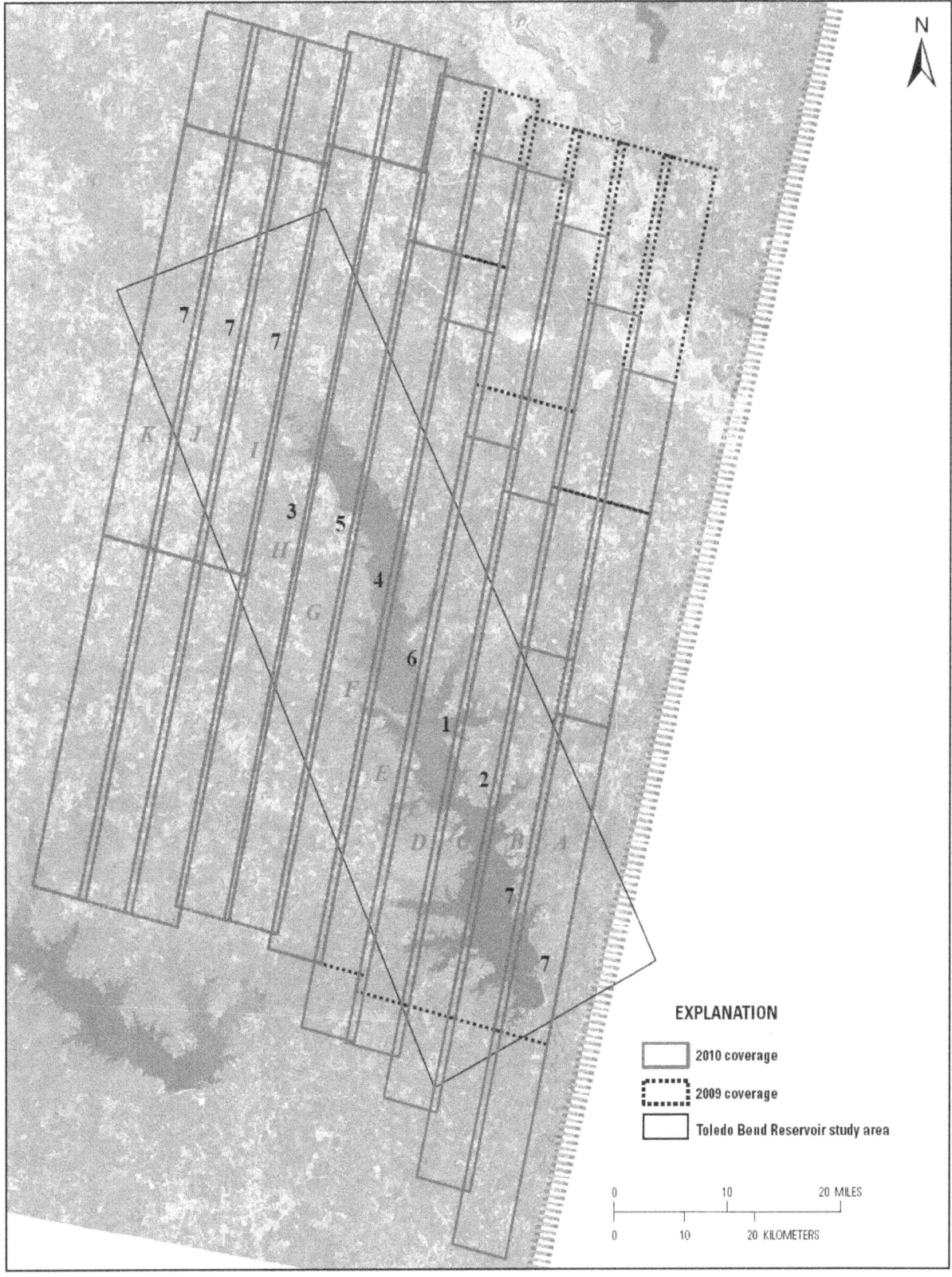

Figure 11. Illustration of the strategy for collecting Hyperion imagery for coverage of lands lying adjacent to the Toledo Bend Reservoir (Louisiana and Texas). Priority zones progressed from 1 as the highest priority to 7 as the lowest. The letters A–K represent the Hyperion image swaths. This graphic represents adjustments that were made to the initial coverage strategy because of timing difficulties and orientation misalignment of the sensor.

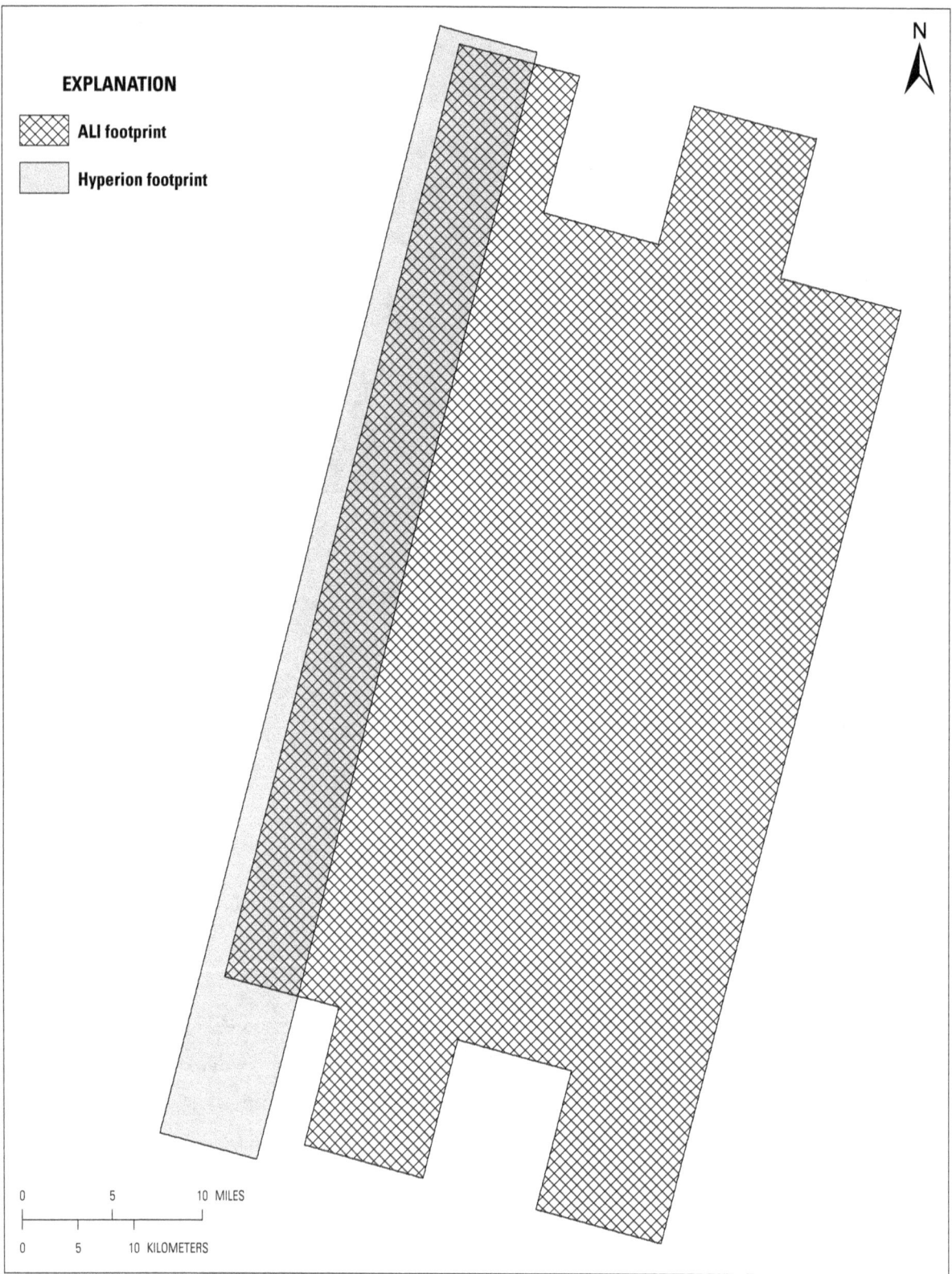

Figure 12. Nominal coverage pattern and relative locations of coverage provided by the Hyperion and Advanced Land Imager (ALI) sensors onboard the Earth Observing-1 satellite. (Example sensor footprints for October 17, 2009.)

Table 2. The set of wavelengths acquired by the Earth Observing-1 Hyperion sensor that was used to map occurrences of Chinese tallow trees (*Triadica sebifera*) within the Toledo Bend Reservoir study area (Louisiana and Texas). The 46 bands highlighted in yellow are the final Hyperion spectral bands used in this study.

Channel	Wavelength	Wavelength center	Channel	Wavelength	Wavelength center	Channel	Wavelength	Wavelength center	Channel	Wavelength	Wavelength center
1	Band-8	0.4268	54	Band-61	0.9629	107	Band-114	1.5581	160	Band-167	2.2845
2	Band-9	0.437	55	Band-62	0.973	108	Band-115	1.5682	161	Band-168	2.2946
3	Band-10	0.4472	56	Band-63	0.9831	109	Band-116	1.5783	162	Band-169	2.3047
4	Band-11	0.4573	57	Band-64	0.9932	110	Band-117	1.5884	163	Band-170	2.3148
5	Band-12	0.4675	58	Band-65	1.0033	111	Band-118	1.5985	164	Band-171	2.3249
6	Band-13	0.4777	59	Band-66	1.0133	112	Band-119	1.6086	165	Band-172	2.335
7	Band-14	0.4879	60	Band-67	1.0234	113	Band-120	1.6187	166	Band-173	2.3451
8	Band-15	0.498	61	Band-68	1.0335	114	Band-121	1.6288	167	Band-174	2.3552
9	Band-16	0.5082	62	Band-69	1.0436	115	Band-122	1.6388			
10	Band-17	0.5184	63	Band-70	1.0537	116	Band-123	1.6489			
11	Band-18	0.5286	64	Band-71	1.0638	117	Band-124	1.659			
12	Band-19	0.5387	65	Band-72	1.0739	118	Band-125	1.6691			
13	Band-20	0.5489	66	Band-73	1.084	119	Band-126	1.6792			
14	Band-21	0.5591	67	Band-74	1.0941	120	Band-127	1.6893			
15	Band-22	0.5693	68	Band-75	1.1042	121	Band-128	1.6994			
16	Band-23	0.5795	69	Band-76	1.1142	122	Band-129	1.7095			
17	Band-24	0.5896	70	Band-77	1.1243	123	Band-130	1.7196			
18	Band-25	0.5998	71	Band-78	1.1344	124	Band-131	1.7297			
19	Band-26	0.61	72	Band-79	1.1445	125	Band-132	1.7397			
20	Band-27	0.6202	73	Band-80	1.1546	126	Band-133	1.7498			
21	Band-28	0.6303	74	Band-81	1.1647	127	Band-134	1.7599			
22	Band-29	0.6405	75	Band-82	1.1748	128	Band-135	1.77			
23	Band-30	0.6507	76	Band-83	1.1849	129	Band-136	1.7801			
24	Band-31	0.6608	77	Band-84	1.195	130	Band-137	1.7902			
25	Band-32	0.671	78	Band-85	1.2051	131	Band-138	1.8003			
26	Band-33	0.6812	79	Band-86	1.2152	132	Band-139	1.9819			
27	Band-34	0.6914	80	Band-87	1.2252	133	Band-140	1.992			
28	Band-35	0.7016	81	Band-88	1.2353	134	Band-141	2.0021			
29	Band-36	0.7117	82	Band-89	1.2454	135	Band-142	2.0324			
30	Band-37	0.7219	83	Band-90	1.2555	136	Band-143	2.0424			
31	Band-38	0.7321	84	Band-91	1.2656	137	Band-144	2.0524			

Table 2. The set of wavelengths acquired by the Earth Observing-1 Hyperion sensor that was used to map occurrences of Chinese tallow trees (*Triadica sebifera*) within the Toledo Bend Reservoir study area (Louisiana and Texas). The 46 bands highlighted in yellow are the final Hyperion spectral bands used in this study. —Continued

Channel	Wavelength	Wavelength center	Channel	Wavelength	Wavelength center	Channel	Wavelength	Wavelength center
32	Band-39	0.7423	85	Band-92	1.2757	138	Band-145	2.0626
33	Band-40	0.7524	86	Band-93	1.2858	139	Band-146	2.0726
34	Band-41	0.7626	87	Band-94	1.2959	140	Band-147	2.0828
35	Band-42	0.7728	88	Band-95	1.306	141	Band-148	2.0928
36	Band-43	0.7829	89	Band-96	1.3161	142	Band-149	2.1029
37	Band-44	0.7931	90	Band-97	1.3261	143	Band-150	2.113
38	Band-45	0.8033	91	Band-98	1.3362	144	Band-151	2.1231
39	Band-46	0.8135	92	Band-99	1.3463	145	Band-152	2.1332
40	Band-47	0.8237	93	Band-100	1.3563	146	Band-153	2.1433
41	Band-48	0.8338	94	Band-101	1.4269	147	Band-154	2.1533
42	Band-49	0.844	95	Band-102	1.437	148	Band-155	2.1634
43	Band-50	0.8542	96	Band-103	1.4471	149	Band-156	2.1735
44	Band-51	0.8644	97	Band-104	1.4572	150	Band-157	2.1836
45	Band-52	0.8745	98	Band-105	1.4673	151	Band-158	2.1937
46	Band-53	0.8847	99	Band-106	1.4774	152	Band-159	2.2038
47	Band-54	0.8949	100	Band-107	1.4875	153	Band-160	2.2139
48	Band-55	0.905	101	Band-108	1.4976	154	Band-161	2.224
49	Band-56	0.9152	102	Band-109	1.5077	155	Band-162	2.2341
50	Band-57	0.9254	103	Band-110	1.5178	156	Band-163	2.2442
51	Band-58	0.9356	104	Band-111	1.5279	157	Band-164	2.2542
52	Band-59	0.9427	105	Band-112	1.5379	158	Band-165	2.2643
53	Band-60	0.9528	106	Band-113	1.548	159	Band-166	2.2744

tallow tree mapping project in 2003 (Ramsey and Nelson, 2005). Although we believe the Hyperion reflectance images provide the best obtainable canopy-reflectance estimates, any deviation in the derived reflectance products, particularly associated with the possible sensor degradations, could not be directly estimated.

Producing Digital Orthographic Mosaics of the Study Area

Digital orthophoto quarter quadrangle (DOQQ) mosaics were created to provide a geographic database for all Hyperion- and ALI-based image rectifications and for visual confirmation of landcover classes used in both the Chinese tallow tree mapping and ALI classifications. The mosaics were created for 2004, 2009, and 2010 to provide a preproject baseline and coverages congruent with Hyperion collections (fig. 13). Mosaic coverages were aligned with the core project area outlined in fig. 11. Mosaics were created with PCI Geomatica software (PCI Geomatics, 1998). The collection dates, numbers, and color-combination rendition of the photographic frames used to create the individual DOQQs are listed in table 3. All other pertinent details concerning the DOQQ sources, accuracy criteria, and mosaic construction are included in the associated metadata file.

Classifying Land Cover of the Study Area

Purpose of Classification Map

The purpose of creating a classification map of landcover was to better link detected occurrences of Chinese tallow tree to land classes (for example, pines versus hardwoods) and human activities (such as the silviculture cycle), as well as to provide a baseline classification of the project area pertinent to the time of mapping. In this case, successful detection of Chinese tallow tree required identifying a spectral reflectance signature uniquely associated with its occurrences. Restricting the spectral variability by applying the detection procedure per landcover class (versus allowing for the entire spectral variance of Chinese tallow tree among all landcover classes) would theoretically facilitate the identification of its unique spectral reflectance signature. Reduction of input spectral variability has been shown to enhance performance of spectral discrimination (Ramsey and Laine, 1997).

Classification of Land Covers on Advanced Land Imager Data

The ALI sensor offered near simultaneous coverage of the entire project area, thus minimizing classification nonconformities caused by changes in vegetation phenology. This minimization was particularly important because the primary collection timeframe for Hyperion data was within the transitional late fall to early winter seasons. The ALI sensor provided sufficient spectral information for discriminating the most prominent land classes. Importantly, ALI data were collected simultaneously with Hyperion data to ensure absolute conformity between vegetation conditions represented in the two types of imagery.

Classification involved four general steps that followed procedures outlined in Ramsey and others (2001; additional pertinent classification details are included in the associated metadata file).The four steps are as follows:

1. Classifications were performed separately on the northern (November 6, 2009) and southern (November 11, 2009) ALI coverages (see fig. 14).

2. Classification was performed by using the PCI Geomatica program suite (PCI Geomatica, 1998). An Iterative Unsupervised Isodata routine was used to create 150 similar spectral clusters.

3. The spectral clusters were assigned class memberships based on comparisons with reconnaissance data and DOQQ mosaics. An enhanced spectral discriminator routine was employed to maximize classification performance (Ramsey and others, 2001).

4. The classification did not follow USGS map protocols or produce summary class accuracies because it was constructed to merely provide necessary information to advance the detection of Chinese tallow tree and associate the Chinese tallow tree with landcover classes and human activities.

Creating Rectified Advanced Land Imager Images for the Landcover Classification

Classifying the ALI images was not a straightforward process. Each ALI spectral band (of which there were nine) and spectral bank (of which there were four) (table 4) had to be separately rectified to the DOQQ mosaics. All bands within a bank were misaligned, and the shift between consecutive bands was not consistent, as shown in figure 15. A general description of the rectification steps is provided below (additional pertinent rectification details are entered into the associated metadata file):

1. Each band had to be separately rectified, resulting in there being 36 separate rectifications per ALI image.

2. After all 36 bands were rectified, the 9 bands common to each bank were regrouped.

3. The four regrouped, orthorectified banks were mosaiced to reconstruct the single ALI image.

4. Complete coverage of the Toledo Bend Reservoir study area required two ALI images. Seventy-two separate rectifications had to be completed and ALI mosaics reconstructed before the landcover classifications could be performed.

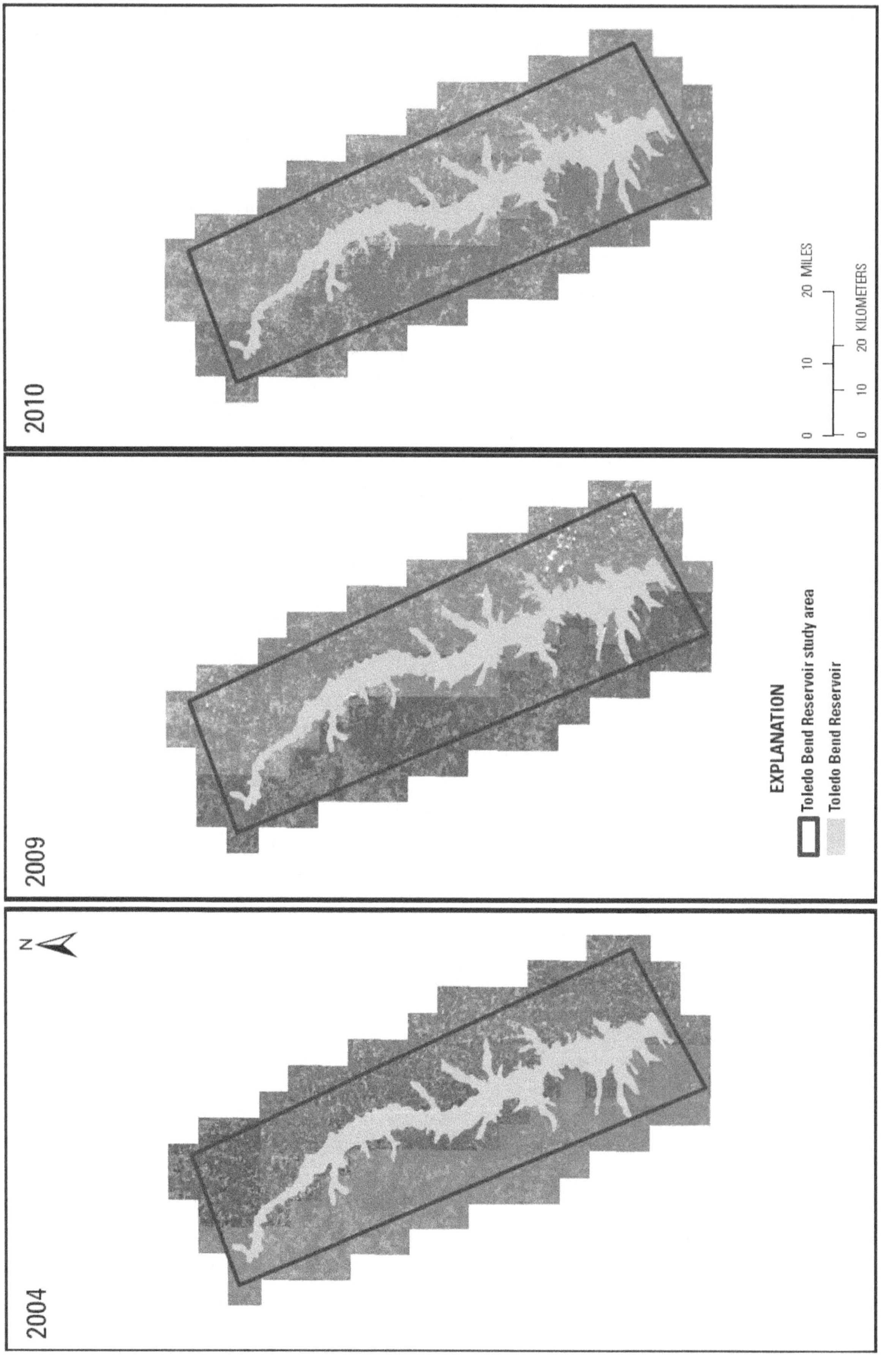

Figure 13. Extents of 2004, 2009, and 2010 digital orthophoto quarter quadrangle mosaics.

Table 3. Characteristics of the digital orthophoto quarter quadrangles spanning the Toledo Bend Reservoir study area (Louisiana and Texas) that were used to provide a geographic database for all Hyperion and ALI based image rectifications.

[DOQQ, digital orthophoto quarter quadrangle; m, meter; CIR, color-infrared; NAIP, National Agriculture Imagery Program; TNRIS, Texas Natural Resources Information System]

	Year	Resolution	Acquisition	Provided as	Obtained from	Number of DOQQ tiles
Louisiana	2004	1 m	winter	CIR	NAIP	76
	2009	1 m	January	True color		76
	2010	1 m	May–August	True color		
Texas	2004	1 m	December	CIR	TNRIS	82
	2009	0.5 m	January	True color		93
	2010	1 m	Leaf-on (entire State observed April–September)	True color		

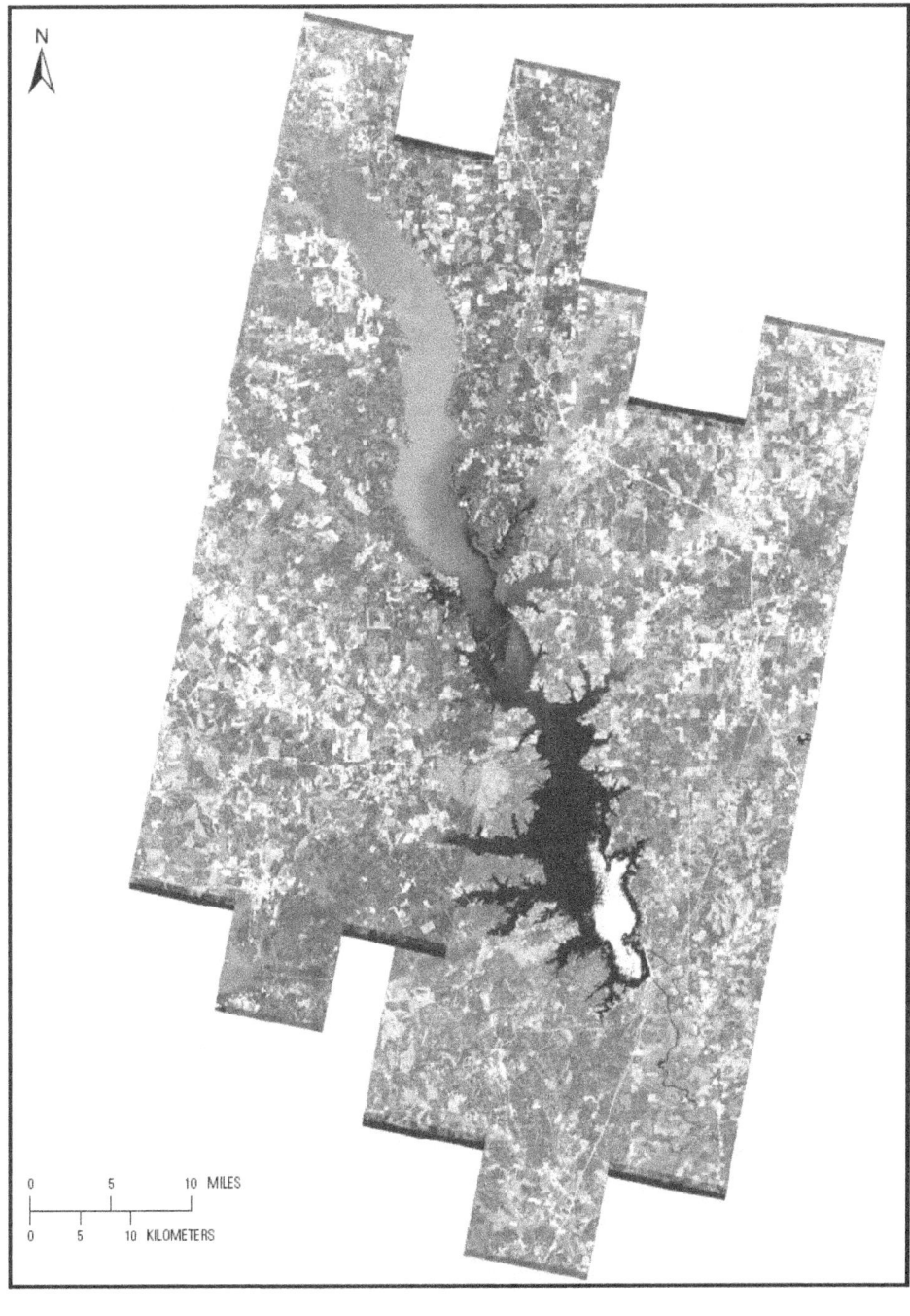

0   5   10 MILES

0   5   10 KILOMETERS

Figure 14. False-color composite mosaic, covering the Toledo Bend Reservoir study area, created by using bands 6, 4, and 3 of two Advanced Land Imager scenes.

Table 4. Orthorectification of banks and bands in Advanced Land Imager imagery.

[ALI, Advanced Land Imager]

ALI orthorectification process			
Raw data	Orthorectify	Merge	Mosaic
Bank 1	Band 1	oBank1	Orthorectified ALI image Oct. 17, 2009
	Band 2		
	Band 3		
	Band 4		
	Band 5		
	Band 6		
	Band 7		
	Band 8		
	Band 9		
Bank 2	Band 1	oBank2	
	Band 2		
	Band 3		
	Band 4		
	Band 5		
	Band 6		
	Band 7		
	Band 8		
	Band 9		
Bank 3	Band 1	oBank3	
	Band 2		
	Band 3		
	Band 4		
	Band 5		
	Band 6		
	Band 7		
	Band 8		
	Band 9		
Bank 4	Band 1	oBank4	
	Band 2		
	Band 3		
	Band 4		
	Band 5		
	Band 6		
	Band 7		
	Band 8		
	Band 9		

Conducting Field Reconnaissance

The primary objective of the study was to locate Chinese tallow tree occurrences in the Toledo Bend Reservoir study area. In a previous mapping project of Chinese tallow tree in southwestern Louisiana, we found that occurrences were not uniformly distributed across the landscape but were differentially distributed across land classes and associated with agriculture and silviculture activities (Ramsey and others, 2005b). Based on that previous experience, we conducted ground-based (November 5–21, 2009; October 28–31, 2010; November 5–8, 2010; and December 20–22, 2010) and aerial helicopter (November 19, 2009) and fixed-wing airplane (November 4–5, 2010) (see table 5) reconnaissance of the study area for two purposes. First, the reconnaissance provided locations of Chinese tallow tree occurrences and an indication of its established spatial pattern and density across the landscape. Secondly, it provided familiarity of the land class coverages (compositions), their spatial distributions, and their structural variability, and it indicated whether Chinese tallow tree was selectively associated with certain land classes or human activities. In addition, during the reconnaissance we attempted to visit all observed Chinese tallow tree sites provided by the Toledo Bend Authority (fig. 16).

Follow-up ground-based reconnaissance surveys were conducted to add validation sites (based on local knowledge) of Chinese tallow tree occurrences and visual observations of associated land-class distributions. Aerial surveys were added to widen the breadth of ground-based observations and permit observations in inaccessible land tracts. The surveys occurred within the Hyperion collection time period but not necessarily concurrent with any one image collection date. A list of ground and aerial surveys by date is included in table 5.

Creating a Hyperlink for Interactive Query of Site-Based Reconnaissance Information

All site information compiled during the ground-based, helicopter, and fixed-wing reconnaissance activities was entered into a constructed interactive database that is available from the Web index page of this report. Each location was linked to the information contained in the site-summary catalogue and is retrievable interactively through a hyperlinked map product. The hyperlinked product provides a visual presentation of the site picture(s), the geographic location, and the nature of the remotely sensed target.

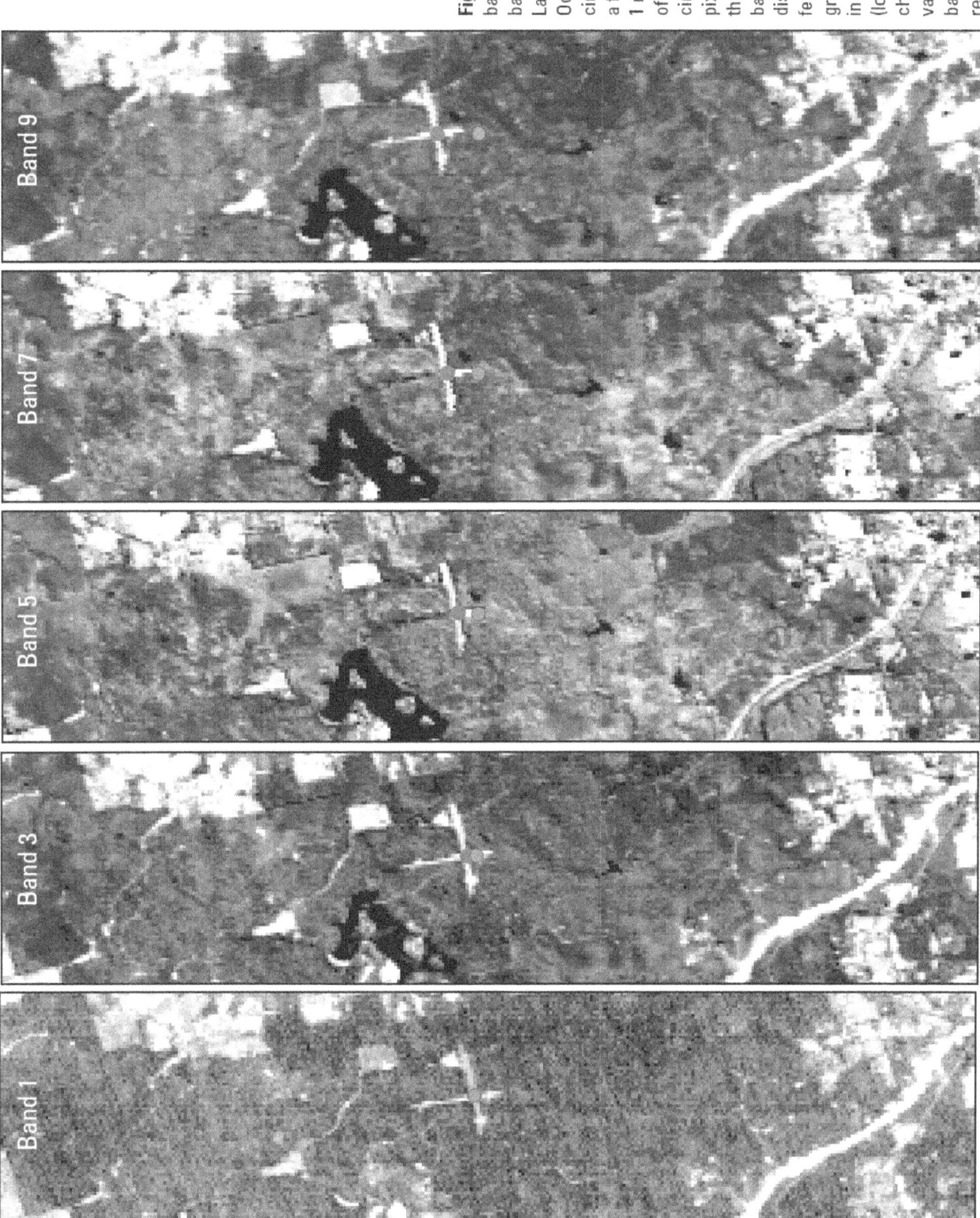

Figure 15. Misalignment from band to band within a single bank (bank 1) of an Advanced Land Imager image from October 17, 2009. The green circle locates the center of a feature as it exists in band 1 relative to the other bands of the same bank. The green circle remains at a constant pixel and row location throughout the series. As the band number increases, the distance between the band 1 feature center (located by the green circle) and its location in subsequent band centers (located by the red circle) changes. This nonsystematic variation meant that each band in each bank had to be rectified separately.

Table 5. List of field reconnaissance surveys conducted for mapping occurrences of Chinese tallow trees (*Triadica sebifera*) within the Toledo Bend Reservoir study area (Louisiana and Texas).

[No., number]

Date	No. of people	Field activities
November 5, 2009	2	Reconnaissance
November 6, 2009	2	Reconnaissance
November 7, 2009	2	Reconnaissance
November 8, 2009	2	Reconnaissance
November 17, 2009	4	Leaf samples, reconnaissance
November 18, 2009	4	Leaf samples, reconnaissance
November 19, 2009	2	Helicopter survey, Reconnaissance
	2	Hemispherical photography, downwelling sunlight recordings, reconnaissance
November 20, 2009	4	Leaf samples, reconnaissance
November 21, 2009	4	Leaf samples, reconnaissance
October 28, 2010	2	Reconnaissance
October 29, 2010	2	Reconnaissance
October 30, 2010	2	Reconnaissance
October 31, 2010	2	Reconnaissance
November 4, 2010	3	Fixed-wing plane survey
Morning November 5, 2010	3	Fixed-wing plane survey
Afternoon November 5, 2010	2	Reconnaissance
November 6, 2010	2	Reconnaissance
November 7, 2010	2	Reconnaissance
November 8, 2010	2	Reconnaissance
December 20, 2010	3	Calibration of oil platforms
December 21, 2010	3	Calibration of oil platforms
December 22, 2010	3	Calibration of oil platforms

Conducting the Helicopter Survey

The objective of the helicopter survey was to gather canopy-reflectance spectra for known vegetation compositions. In turn, these spectra were used for calibration of Hyperion-based spectral indicators of Chinese tallow tree and validation of mapping performance (Ramsey and others, 2005a). The helicopter survey included validation sites selected in previously conducted ground surveys.

Collection of useable reflected sunlight (upwelling) spectra of selected canopies required an almost stationary helicopter platform located at a nearly constant aboveground or canopy level. Stability was required so that the handheld radiometer used to measure the reflected sunlight (upwelling) was kept at a near constant nadir orientation and altitude during the collection of up to six replicate spectra at each site. Simultaneous to the helicopter-based upwelling collections, sun illumination (downwelling) of the surface (or canopy) was collected with a fully diffuse and hemispherical stationary sensor positioned within the coverage area of the helicopter survey (for example, fig. 7). Unfortunately, stabilization difficulties during the helicopter survey severely limited the useable upwelling spectra, and a delay in the helicopter launch time restricted the downwelling collection period. Working within those limitations, spectra judged to be acceptable were processed following Ramsey and others (2005a). Canopy reflectance spectra were calculated from the upwelling to downwelling spectral ratio (fig. 8). In essence, the canopy reflectance is simply the amount of reflected sunlight from a canopy, divided by the amount of sunlight illuminating the canopy. By creating the ratio of these two measurements, an intrinsic reflectance estimate of the canopy is created. All passive sensor systems solely measure the reflected sunlight or upwelling light, thus providing only relative measures. Intrinsic properties will not vary with changes in sun illumination, view orientation (satellite and aircraft sensor and target geometry), or atmospheric transparency (for example, haze and clouds). An intrinsic property only changes if the target changes (for instance, a change in the canopy composition).

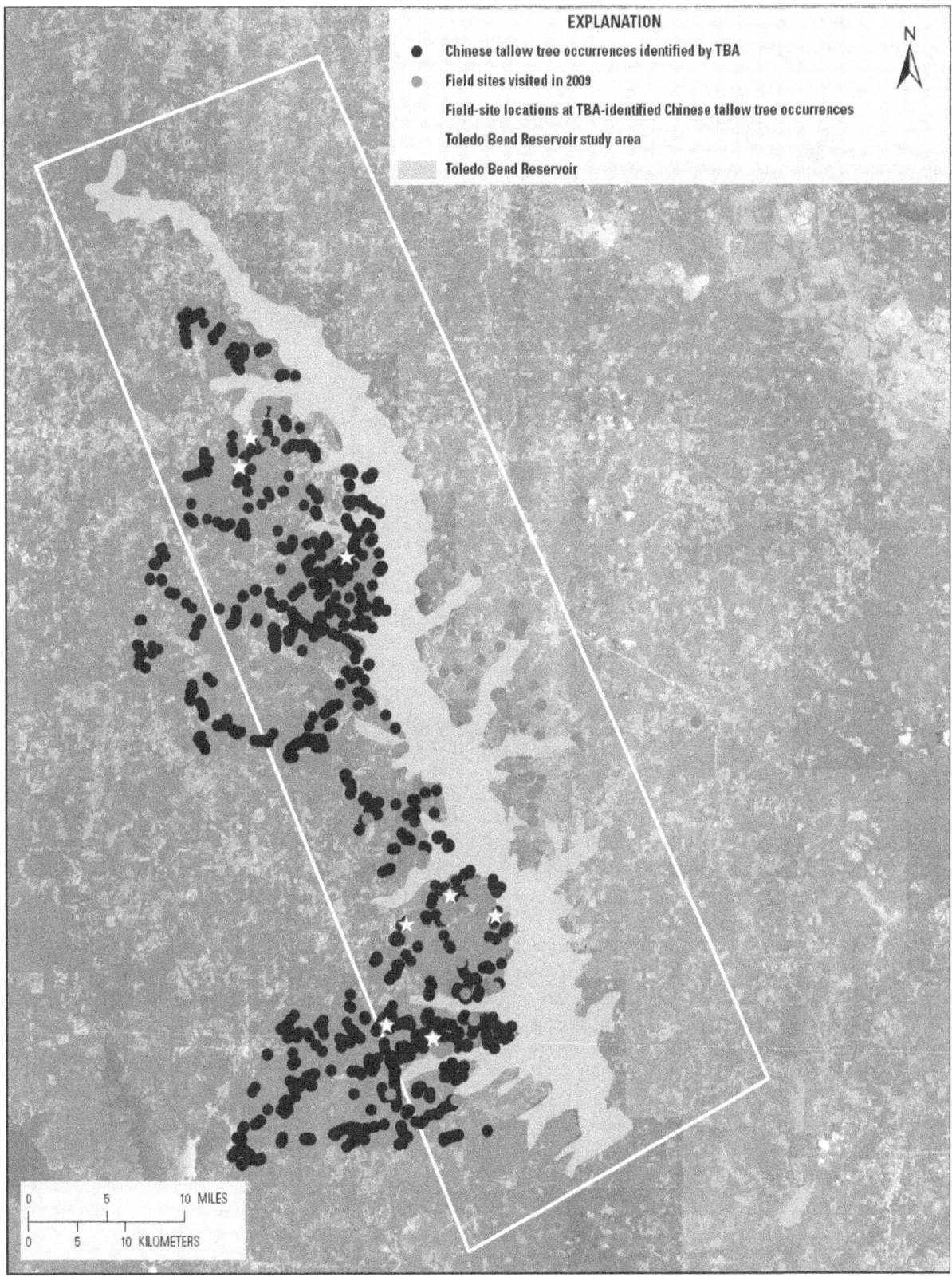

Figure 16. Locations of Chinese tallow tree (*Triadica sebifera*) occurrences received from personnel of the Toledo Bend Authority (TBA) at the project initiation (black circles).

Laboratory Measurements of Leaf Spectral Properties

During the ground-based reconnaissance, we found that several tree species and one shrub species exhibited similar senescing foliage as did Chinese tallow tree. Because successful mapping of Chinese tallow tree occurrences depended upon the uniqueness of its red-leaf foliage in the landscape, spectral measurements of leaves were obtained in order to determine the spectral contrast between those of Chinese tallow tree and those of all other co-occurring plants within the project area (for example, fig. 2). Small branches were collected from Chinese tallow, red maple (*Acer rubrum*), and sweetgum (*Liquidambar styraciflua*) trees during the ground surveys, and these were analyzed within 24 hours. The leaf samples included green, yellow, and red leaves and leaves exhibiting progressive color changes between these dominant colors. Leaf-reflectance spectra were obtained by using a handheld radiometer fitted with a diffuse sample sphere. The various spectral measurements and replicates were entered into postprocessing algorithms that calculated the average diffuse reflectance for each leaf. Full details concerning the measurement methods and postprocessing analyses may be found in Ramsey and others (2005b).

Nonvegetated Calibration and Validation Targets

Using Nonvegetated Targets for Calibration

Nonvegetated targets were included within the spectral calibration dataset in order to provide a more spatially uniform and spectrally stable surface than possible with vegetated canopies (fig. 17). This increased uniformity and stability enhanced the performance of the atmospheric correction process, and thereby, the accuracy of the produced canopy-reflectance images. The nonvegetated targets consisted entirely of oil-well platforms that were predominantly located in the northern half of the project area; however, some exist in the southern region as well. The existence of oil-well platform sites was discovered during the 2010 fixed-wing reconnaissance flights (fig. 18). Permission for access to the oil-well platforms from Swift Energy Operating, LLC (Houston, Tex.) and Chesapeake Operating, Inc. (Oklahoma City, Okla.) was granted soon after the completion of the fixed-wing reconnaissance.

Creating Calibration Spectra from Nonvegetated Sources

We collected 10–20 ground-based upwelling and associated downwelling spectra sets at random locations within a 60- to 90-m area of each oil-well platform where the ground surface within the platform area exhibited fairly good composition and weathering uniformity. The ground-surface spectra were collected with a handheld radiometer (please refer to the "Conducting the Helicopter Survey" section on handheld radiometer collection and spectral definition) at a height of 1 m above the ground surface with a 15° aperture. At that height, the ground spatial area or field of view was 26 centimeters in length defining a maximum ground field-of-view of 0.068 square meters (m²). Next, four to six downwelling sunlight-illumination spectra were collected from an 18 percent grey card immediately after the completion of the upwelling spectra collection at each location in the selected platform area. The grey card was held horizontal to the platform ground surface (Ramsey and Jensen, 1995).

The individual means for the upwelling and downwelling spectra at each location were calculated and the errors about the means calculated. The mean reflectance spectrum was calculated as the ratio of the upwelling and downwelling means for each location within the platform, and the error about mean was calculated by combining the mean errors for the upwelling and downwelling spectra. Finally, the mean and propagated error spectra (for each location) were combined to produce a calibration mean and error spectra for each calibration target site.

Deriving Indicator Spectra for Chinese Tallow Tree

Vegetated site locations within the Hyperion reflectance images that were to be used for calibration and validation of the produced Chinese tallow tree occurrence maps were primarily selected from the reconnaissance points. Site selections relied on observed locations of Chinese tallow trees within each Hyperion image and from land classes defined in the classified ALI images. For instance, sites associated with the "bottomland hardwood" class would contain both sites with observed Chinese tallow trees and sites without Chinese tallow trees. Selected reconnaissance sites were first located on the DOQQ mosaics and the ALI-based landcover map and then on the nonrectified Hyperion reflectance images. The nonrectified Hyperion images were used to avoid spectral averaging that occurs during the rectification processing.

Extracting Hyperion Spectral Data

Extracting the composite reflectance spectrum from each Hyperion reflectance image was accomplished by using a PCI Geomatica procedure (PCI Geomatics, 1998). The number of pixels comprising each extracted mean spectrum varied, dependent on the vegetation makeup of the targeted site. Single-pixel extractions were normally associated with ground or helicopter locations. These Hyperion reflectance datasets were catalogued by land class and the presence or absence of Chinese tallow trees.

Initially all spectra extracted from the Hyperion reflectance image were combined in the dataset input to the PVA software suite (Ehrlich, 2000). Because of some swath-to-swath variability in reflectance estimates, the datasets were

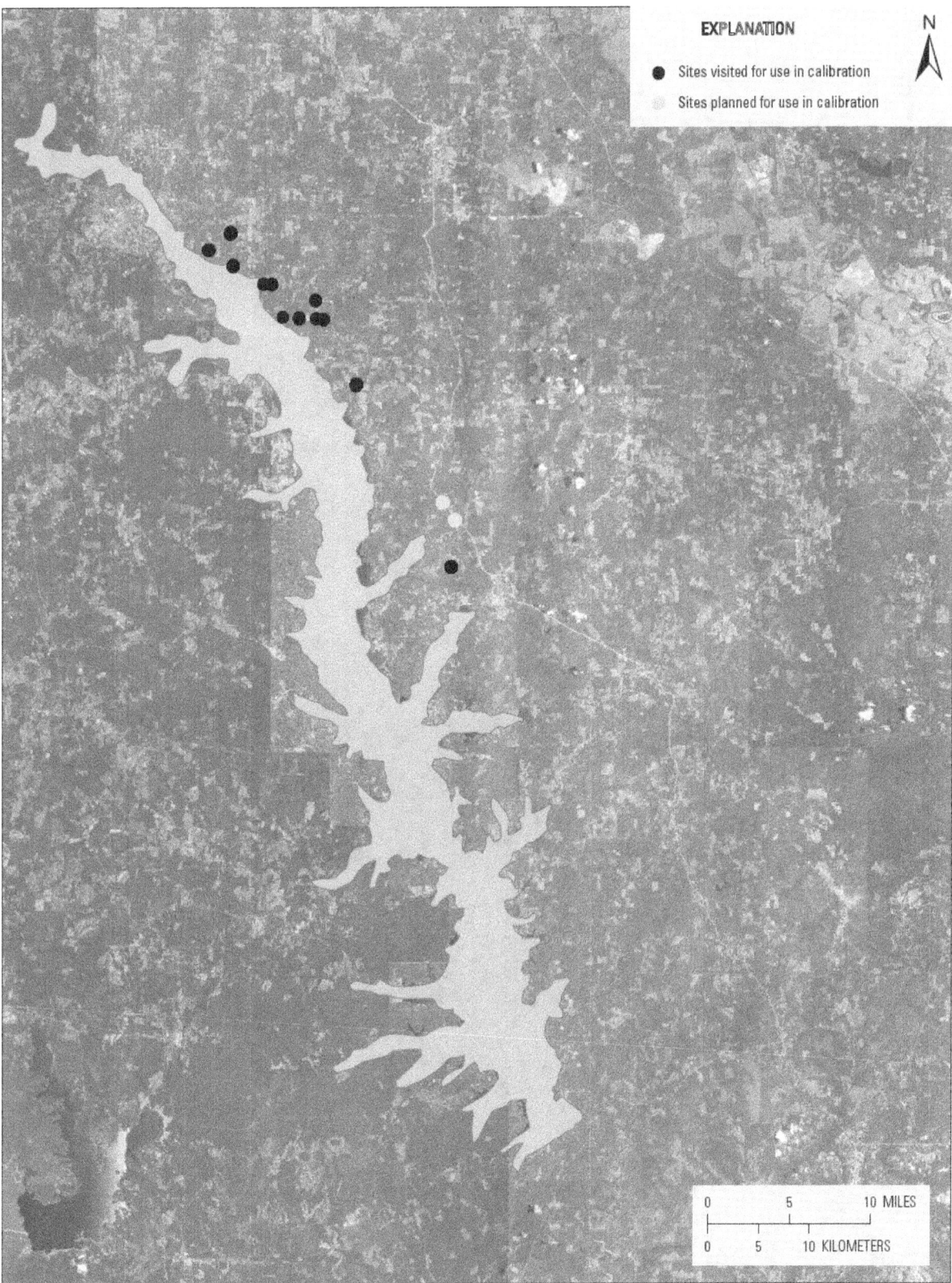

Figure 17. Ground-based field sites visited or planned for use in calibrating atmospherically corrected Hyperion reflectance images (only a subset of the planned sites could be visited because of lacking access permissions).

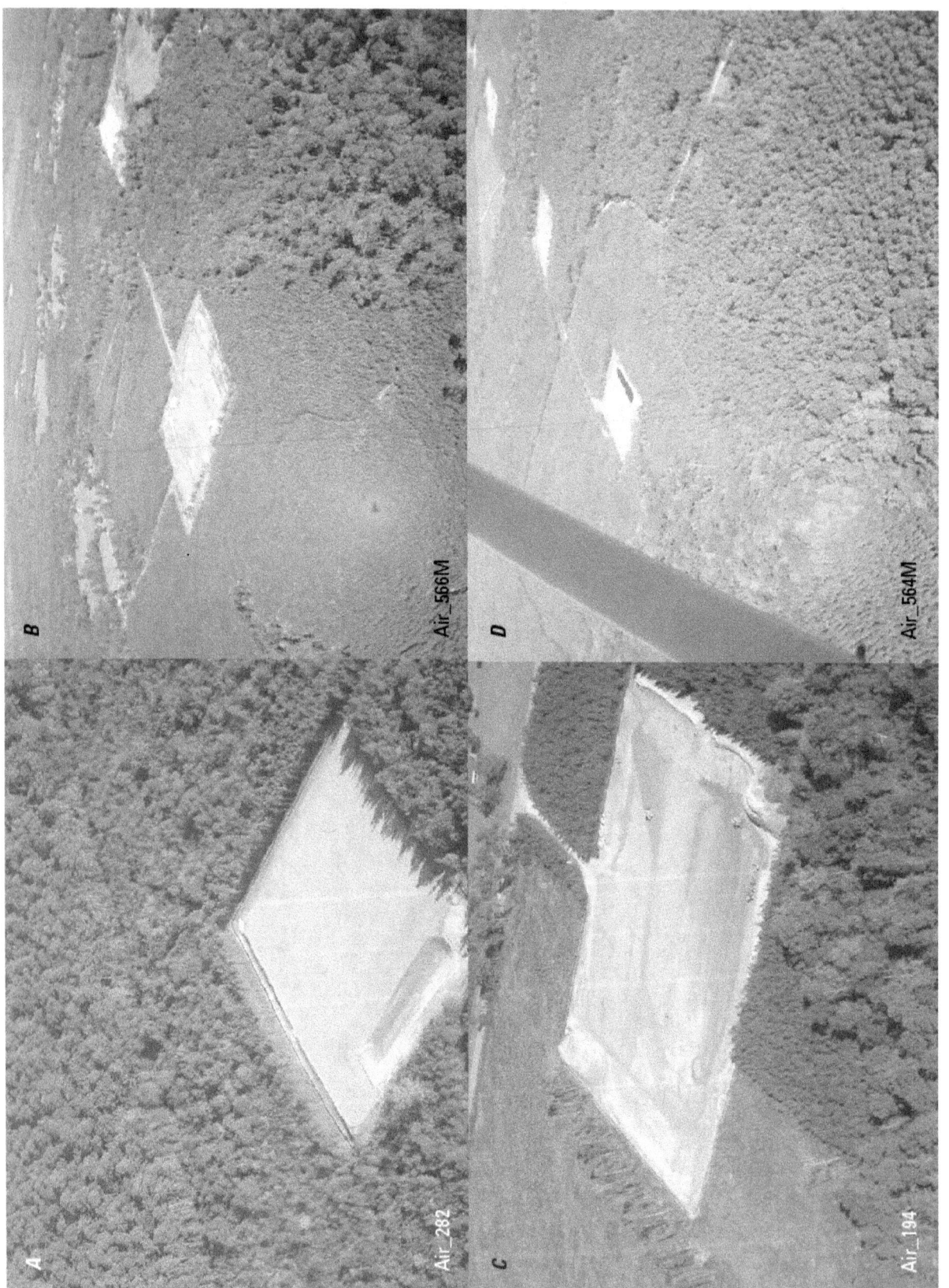

Figure 18. Oil-well platforms were used as nonvegetated calibration sites (see fig. 17 for platform locations). Oil platforms at different stages of construction and length of service. *A*, fresh gravel; *B*, in use for unknown period; *C*, under construction, dirt layer before gravel addition; *D*, in use for unknown period. The name, for example Air_282, on the photograph indicates the site name, and more details of the sites can be obtained from the interactive query database available at the Web index page of this report.

constructed by swath and date. The reflectance dataset was entered into a formatted data file and processed with PVA software as described in Ramsey and others (2005b). If PVA failed to discriminate the Chinese tallow tree from the non-Chinese tallow tree sites in the full dataset, input datasets were separated by land class or by selected combinations of land classes (for example, mixed pines and hardwood stands).

Creating Indicator Spectra from the Helicopter-Based Reflectance Dataset

In addition to calibration and validation spectra extracted directly from the Hyperion reflectance images, useable canopy-reflectance spectra obtained during the helicopter survey were entered into the PVA. The purpose of analyzing this dataset was to determine if a well-conditioned indicator spectrum for Chinese tallow tree reflectance could be identified from the available canopy-reflectance spectra. Indicator spectra from the reflectance dataset obtained by helicopter were combined with each Hyperion calibration and validation dataset. By including the indicator spectra derived from the helicopter dataset we hoped to enhance the PVA performance. Enhanced performance was judged on whether or not sites of known or suspected Chinese tallow tree occurrence, and conversely sites known or suspected to be without Chinese tallow tree occurrence, were properly identified within the PVA results.

Applying PolyVector Analysis-Derived Indicator Spectra to the Hyperion Reflectance Image

Promising indicator spectra identified by PVA were reformatted as standard ASCII II data files and entered into the PCI Geomatica SPUNMIX procedure. SPUNMIX operated individually on each pixel in the Hyperion reflectance image. Each canopy reflectance spectrum of each pixel was apportioned a weighted combination of input indicator spectra whose linear combination best replicated the composite reflectance spectra or the canopy reflectance spectrum of each Hyperion pixel. The resultant weighting of each input indicator spectrum (normalized to 100 percent) was mapped to the target pixel. At the end of the SPUNMIX application, each pixel in the Hyperion reflectance image was transformed to a continuous variable reflecting the percent occurrence of each indicator reflectance spectrum, and a real image was output for each indicator spectra. The real image files output by SPUNMIX were rectified to the appropriate DOQQ mosaic.

Overlaying Predicted Chinese Tallow Tree Occurrences onto the Landcover Map

The georectified map of Chinese tallow tree occurrences output by SPUNMIX was overlain on the ALI-based landcover map. The spatial distribution of Chinese tallow tree occurrences produced by the SPUNMIX program was examined for consistency with known and likely Chinese tallow tree occurrences.

Results

Hyperion and Advanced Land Imager Coverages

Hyperion Coverages

Hyperion images covering the project area were collected in 2009 (22 images), 2010 (19 images), and 2011 (10 images) (table 6). The 2011 collections were in late winter (January and February). Of these collections, the useable Hyperion images are identified by color shading in figure 19. "Useable" refers to images that met the following criteria: (1) aligned with the swath-template pattern of orientation from northeast to southwestern and (2) free of cloud and cloud shadow contamination. Not listed in table 6 are those Hyperion collections that were scheduled but not collected because of scheduling difficulties and priority overrides.

In total, there were 29 useable Hyperion images collected from 2009 to 2011. Stratified by coverage swath (fig. 19), the majority of useable Hyperion image collections were concentrated in the highest priority swaths identified by Toledo Bend Reservoir personnel. Because detection is based on the green-to-red color change of Chinese tallow tree senescing leaves, the Hyperion image collections that occurred from October through December were the most important with respect to detection. In total, there were 20 useable Hyperion images collected within the time frame of senescence, with frequencies per swath ranging from 1 to 5. Hyperion images collected within the highest priority swaths during fall to early winter senescence were the first processed.

Advanced Land Imager Coverages

Only useable ALI images were used in the calculation of coverage frequency per swath, with "useable" defined as it was in relation to the Hyperion imagery. The useable ALI images matched the dates of the useable Hyperion images (table 6). The highest frequency of ALI coverage was centered on the southern portion of the project area. Similarly, the highest Hyperion coverages were centered over the southern section; however, a single swath in the northern section of the Toledo Bend Reservoir also had high coverage. This slight geographic discrepancy in coverage frequency between the Hyperion and ALI sensors was because of the alignment of the Hyperion swath on the western edge of the ALI coverage as part of the simultaneous collections of the Hyperion and ALI sensors.

Table 6. List of image collections by the Advanced Land Imager and Hyperion sensors aboard the Earth Observing-1 satellite that were used for mapping Chinese tallow tree (*Triadica sebifera*) in the Toledo Bend Reservoir study area (Louisiana and Texas). The light grey shades on the table show unusable images with high cloud cover; the dark grey shades show satellite data not acquired by the National Aeronautics and Space Administration (NASA).

[ID, identification; ALI, Advanced Land Imager; %, percent]

Month	Day	Image ID (ALI)	Cloud	Hyperion swath[1]	ALI[2]	Hyperion[3]
			2009			
October	14	EO10240382009287110	80–89%	1D	Cloudy	Cloudy
	17	EO10240382009290110	0–9 %	1D	Clear	Clear
	19	EO10250382009292110	0–9 %	3H	Clear	Clear
	27	EO10240382009300110	90–100 %	2C	Cloudy	Cloudy
November	1	Cancelled by NASA	0–9 %	2C		
	4	EO10240382009308110	0–9 %	2C	Clear	Clear
	6	EO10250382009310110	0–9 %	3H	Clear	Clear
	11	EO10240382009315110	0–9 %	1D	Clear	Clear
	14	EO10250382009318110	70–79%	4F	Partly cloudy	Partly cloudy
	17	EO10250382009321110	60–69%	3H	Cloudy	Cloudy
	19	EO10250382009323110	20–29%	5G	Partly cloudy	Partly cloudy
	22	EO10250382009326110	90–100%	4F	Cloudy	Cloudy
	24	EO10240382009328110	90–100%	1D	Cloudy	Cloudy
	27	Cancelled by NASA	10–19%	1D		
December	2	EO10240382009336110	90–100%	1D	Cloudy	Cloudy
	5	EO10250382009339110	0–9 %	3H	Clear	Clear
	7	EO10240382009341110	90–100%	1D	Cloudy	Cloudy
	10	EO10250382009344110	50–59%	7I	Partly cloudy	Partly cloudy
	12	EO10240382009346110	90–100%	1D	Cloudy	Cloudy
	15	EO10240382009349110	90–100%	1D	Cloudy	Cloudy
	18	EO10250382009352110	0–9 %	7I	Clear	Clear
	20	EO10240382009354110	0–9 %	1D	Clear	Clear
	23	EO10240382009357110	90–100%	2C	Cloudy	Cloudy
	25	EO10250382009359110	0–9%	6E	Clear	Clear
			2010			
January	2	Cancelled by NASA	0–9%	2C		
	5	EO10250382010005110	0–9%	4F	Clear	Clear
	7	EO10250382010007110	90–100%	5G	Cloudy	Cloudy
	10	EO10240382010010110	0–9%	2C	Clear	Clear
	12	EO10250382010012110	0–9%	5G	Clear	Clear
	15	Cancelled by NASA	90–100%	1D	Cloudy	Cloudy
	17	EO10240382010017110	60–69%	1D	Cloudy	Cloudy
	23	EO10250382010023110	90–100%	3H	Cloudy	Cloudy
	25	EO10240382010025110	0–9%	1D	Clear	Clear
October	8	EO10250382010281110	0–9%	6E	Clear	Clear
	13	EO10240382010286110	0–9%	1D	Clear	Clear
	15	EO10240382010288110	0–9%	2C	Clear	Clear
	18	EO10250382010291110	20–29%	4F	Partly cloudy	Partly cloudy
	23	Cancelled by NASA		5G		

Table 6.   List of image collections by the Advanced Land Imager and Hyperion sensors aboard the Earth Observing-1 satellite that were used for mapping Chinese tallow tree (*Triadica sebifera*) in the Toledo Bend Reservoir study area (Louisiana and Texas). The light grey shades on the table show unusable images with high cloud cover; the dark grey shades show satellite data not acquired by the National Aeronautics and Space Administration (NASA).—Continued

[ID, identification; ALI, Advanced Land Imager; %, percent]

Month	Day	Image ID (ALI)	Cloud	Hyperion swath[1]	ALI[2]	Hyperion[3]
November	5	EO10240382010309110	0–9%	1D	Clear	Clear
	10	EO10250382010314110	20–29%	3H	Partly cloudy	cloudy
	18	EO10250382010322110	70–79%	3H	Cloudy	Cloudy
	26	EO10240382010330110	90–100%	7B	Cloudy	Cloudy
	28	EO10250382010332110	10–19%	3H	Partly cloudy	Partly cloudy
December	1	EO10240382010335110	0–9%	2C	Clear	Clear
	19	EO10240382010353110	0–9%	7B	Clear	Clear
	24	EO10250382010358110	40–49%	6E	Partly cloudy	Partly cloudy
		2011				
January	1	EO10250382011001110	90–100%	5G	Cloudy	Cloudy
	6	EO10250382011006110	0–9%	5G	Clear	Clear
	11	EO10250382011011110	0–9%	6E	Clear	Clear
	19	EO10240382011019110	70–80%	1D	Cloudy	Cloudy
	27	EO10240382011027110	0–9%	1D	Clear	Clear
February	6	EO10250382011037110KF	0–9%	4F	Clear	Clear
March	1	EO1A0250382011060110KF	0–9%	4F	Clear	Clear
	9	EO1A0250382011068110KF	30–39%	4F	Partly cloudy	Partly cloudy
	12	EO1A0250382011071110KF	80–89%	6E	Cloudy	Cloudy
	27	EO1A0250382011086110	90–100%	6E	Cloudy	Cloudy

[1]Hyperion swath location shown on figure 11.

[2]Advanced Land Imager (ALI) provides image data from nine spectral bands and one panchromatic band (band designations). The instrument operates in a pushbroom fashion, with a spatial resolution of 30 meters for the multispectral bands and 10 meters for the panchromatic band. The standard scene width is 37 kilometers. Standard scene length is 42 kilometers, with an optional increased scene length of 185 kilometers.

[3]Hyperion collects 220 unique spectral channels ranging from 0.357 to 2.576 micrometers with a 10 nanometer bandwidth. The instrument operates in a pushbroom fashion, with a spatial resolution of 30 meters for all bands. The standard scene width is 7.7 kilometers. Standard scene length is 42 kilometers, with an optional increased scene length of 185 kilometers. U.S. Geological Survey web site http://edcsns17.cr.usgs.gov/eo1/lookAngles.php.

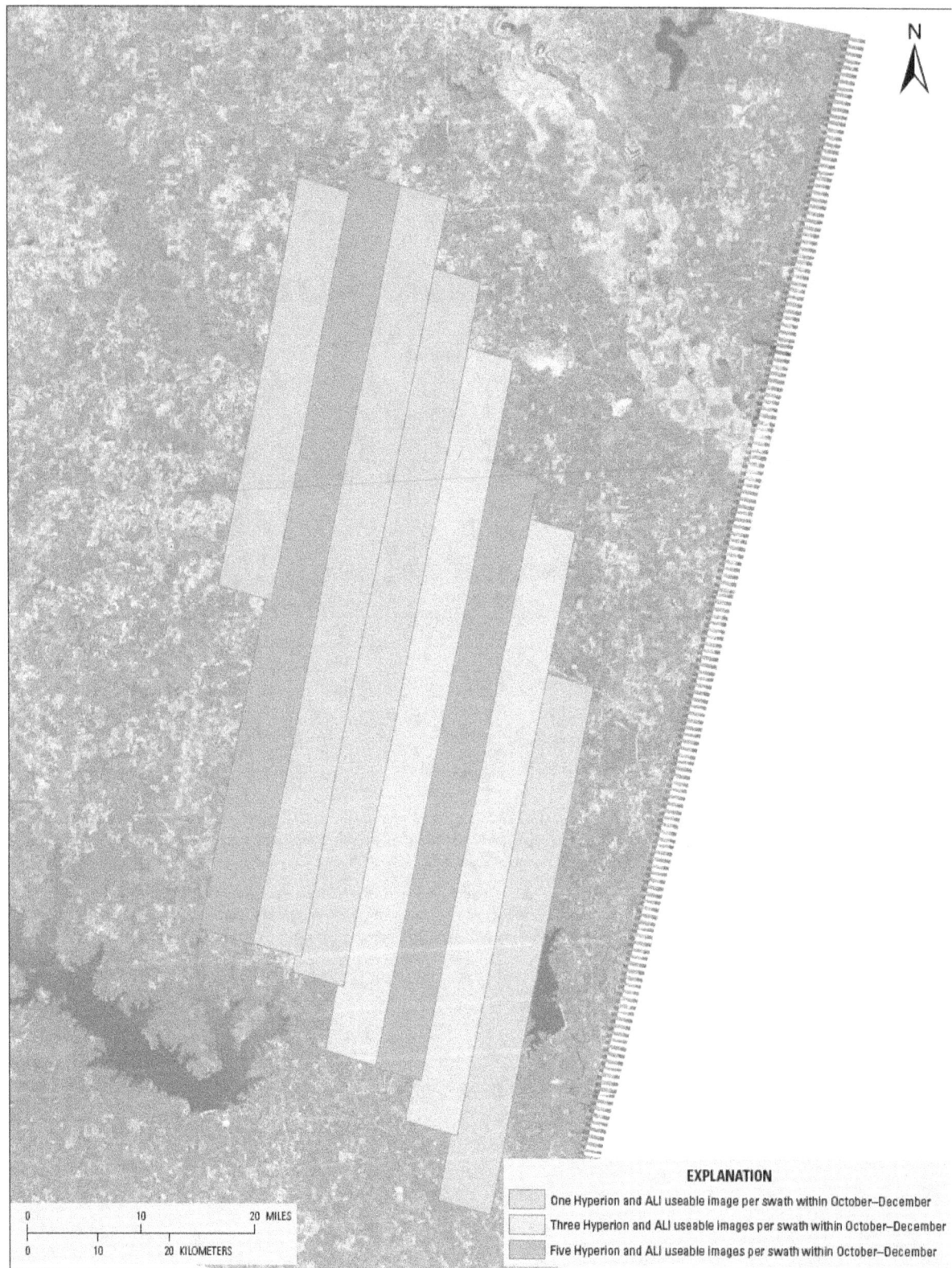

Figure 19.   The number of useable or nearly cloud-free Hyperion images collected per swath during the fall senescent period (October–December) in 2009 to 2010 (see fig. 11 for swath locations and naming conventions).

Field Reconnaissance in Support of Chinese Tallow Tree Mapping

Ground-Based Field Reconnaissance

Ground-based field reconnaissance occurred during 5 time periods from 2009 through 2010 at 226 locations throughout the Toledo Bend Reservoir study area (table 5, fig. 20). Ground-based observations were restricted to accessible lands tracts. This restriction resulted in observations emphasizing edges mainly associated with public roadways, power lines, and areas of transition in forest-stand structure (primarily related to an abrupt transition from planted pine or scrubland to mature forest). There were excursions made into the forested areas; however, the overlapped timing of Chinese tallow tree senescence and hunting seasons severely limited these forays. Where agriculture lands (mostly grasslands for grazing), pine plantations, or scrublands occurred along the roadways, these were observed from the fence line. Observations of low-density development were also emphasized because of accessibility; however, single residences reachable by a private roadway typically were not visited. Public facilities were included in the survey (for example, campgrounds and boat launches). These public locations were where most shoreline observations of the Toledo Bend Reservoir were made. Even though the reconnaissance was not without significant limitations, the ground-based observations provided a sense of the magnitude and distribution of Chinese tallow tree occurrences in the study area.

Observations from Fixed-Wing Aircraft

During fixed-wing aircraft reconnaissance, which occurred on November 4 and 5, 2010, natural-color photographic data were collected at 547 vegetated locations throughout the project area (table 5, fig. 21). All photographs were oblique. In all but a few cases, the nominal direction of the target in the photography was recorded, as well as a general description of the target. To provide a more meaningful fixed-wing observational dataset, the recorded aircraft altitude and nadir position and estimated view angle were used to calculate the ground distance to the intended target feature in each photograph. In cases where the photographic data was judged to be most helpful in encapsulating the information derivable from the fixed-wing photography, the nadir positions of the aircraft were adjusted to more correctly locate the target feature in the photographs. In the photographic archive, an "m" was appended to photographs where target locations were repositioned in the coverage maps. Even though the fixed-wing reconnaissance allowed for more thorough coverage of the study area, it did not allow identification of herbaceous vegetation except into broad categories such as pine and hardwood and a nondescript shrub category. As was also the case in the leaf-reflectance results, differentiation between similarly colored leaves (red or green) of red maple, sweetgum, and Chinese tallow trees was unattainable. Poison sumac (*Toxicodendron vernix*), an herbaceous shrub, may have also been included in observations of red foliage. Because red leaves of the three species could not be distinguished, aerial observations were aggregated into a general "red trees" category.

At some sites where red trees were directly observed during the flight, the associated photography did not substantiate those direct observations. Where direct observations during the flight and (or) results (specific or extrapolated) of the previously conducted ground surveys indicated possible occurrences of Chinese tallow tree (within the "red tree" class), a category of "possible" occurrence was introduced into the mapped results of the fixed-wing aerial survey.

In the fixed-wing aerial reconnaissance senescing hardwoods exhibited foliage tones that seemed, for the most part, visually distinguishable from those of red trees. Understory red trees in mature forests were at times observable, but these occurrences were mainly limited to forest gaps or instances when observations were made from a nearly vertical stance relative to the target (fig. 22A, B). Subcanopy red shrubs and trees were most often observed at edges of transition from pine plantation or scrubland to mature forest. For the most part, these edge-positioned subcanopy occurrences were associated with elongated and narrow hardwood stands surrounded by a pine plantation (fig. 23A, B, and C). Photographs were also collected of land classes that did not include red trees. These photographs were obtained to document the various land classes in the project area; however, photography was predominantly taken when red trees were observed.

Helicopter-Based Observations

In total, vegetation compositions were documented at 12 sites during the helicopter flight on November 19, 2009 (fig. 24). This was the only survey during which near-nadir photographs were collected. This helicopter-based aerial photography provided the only near nadir views of the compositions of various canopies, including Chinese tallow tree occurrences, thus supplementing ground-based observations. In addition, the near nadir sampling simulated the imaging geometries of the Hyperion and ALI sensors, albeit at a much higher spatial resolution (figs. 24 A, B). The helicopter sites included mature and planted pine forests, mixed hardwood stands, and open water. Sites with and without Chinese tallow tree were documented. Helicopter photographic and ground-based canopy composition observations were grouped within the ground observation category.

Spectral Properties of Leaves

Between November 17–21, 2009, 36 leaf samples were collected at 20 sites, including 15 sweetgum, 13 red

Figure 20.   Locations of 226 field sites surveyed during ground reconnaissance for Chinese tallow trees (*Triadica sebifera*) in the Toledo Bend Reservoir study area (Louisiana and Texas). The sites indicated in yellow on the map are those where Chinese tallow tree was observed and the sites marked with green where Chinese tallow tree was not observed.

Figure 21. Results of fixed-wing aerial reconnaissance for Chinese tallow trees (*Triadica sebifera*) in the Toledo Bend Reservoir study area (Louisiana and Texas). A general category of "red trees" is used because red foliage of multiple trees and shrubs were indistinguishable. Where direct observations during the flight and (or) results of a previously conducted ground survey indicated possible occurrences of Chinese tallow tree (within the red tree class), a category of "possible Chinese tallow tree occurrence" was introduced into the mapped results of the fixed-wing aerial survey.

Figure 22. Red-leafed trees and green-leafed Chinese tallow trees (*Triadica sebifera*) in mature pine (*Pinus* L. spp.) forests. *A*, Aerial view of red trees. *B*, Ground view of red trees. *A* and *B* do not depict the same forest stand, and the red tree in *B* is a red maple. *C*, *D*, Green-leafed Chinese tallow trees in a forest dominated by pine but located on the edge of a narrow roadway. The names on the photograph, for example Air_247, indicate the site name, and more details of the sites can be obtained from the interactive query database available at the Web index page of this report.

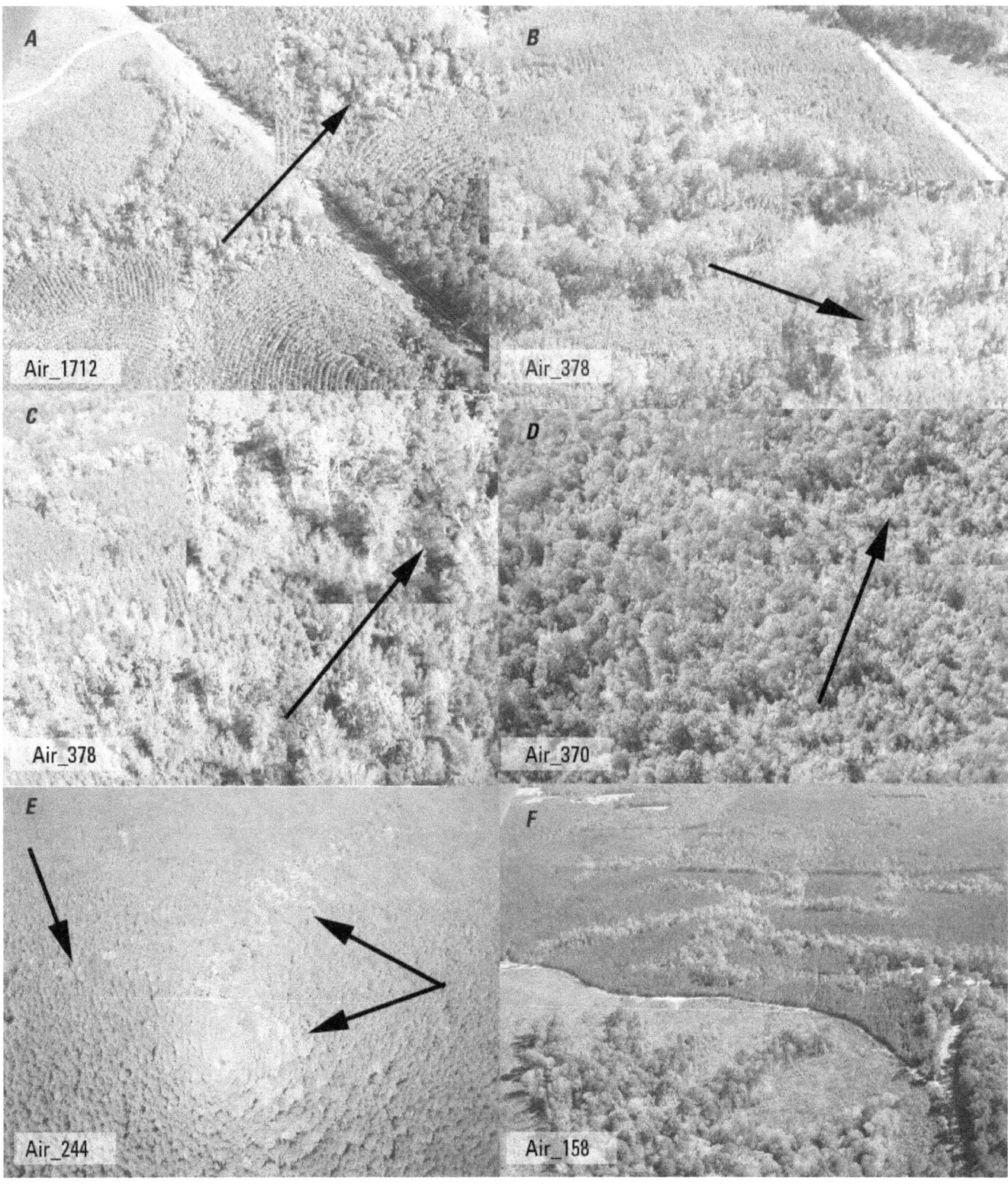

Figure 23. Aerial view of red trees in hardwood forests. *A, B, C,* Red trees and shrubs occupying the understory of hardwood forests (hardwood fingers). *D,* Red trees in a canopy gap of a hardwood, or possibly a mixed hardwood forest and pine stand. *E,* Illustrates the high spectral mixing of the hardwood fingers in the surrounding pine, or mixed pine and hardwood forest. *F,* A clear depiction of the hardwood fingers intertwined in a young pine plantation and recently clear cut area.

Figure 24. Photographs collected during the helicopter survey of the Toledo Bend Reservoir study area (Louisiana and Texas). *A*, Includes two young pine plantations with and without Chinese tallow trees, and a mixed pine and hardwood forest with and without Chinese tallow trees. *B*, Chinese tallow trees observed in canopy gaps and edge of a mixed pine and hardwood forest. The names on the photograph, for example, HS1_M, indicate the site name, and more details of the sites can be obtained from the interactive query database available at the Web index page of this report.

maple, and 8 Chinese tallow tree. A mean transmittance and reflectance spectrum was obtained for each leaf sample. Figure 25 shows an example of the green, yellow, and red leaves of Chinese tallow, red maple, and sweetgum trees.

Green, red, and yellow Chinese tallow tree leaves spatially co-occurred within the project area. As seen in figure 26, most often the reflectance from red and yellow leaves contrast sharply with green Chinese tallow tree leaves. Reflectance spectra associated with red-leaf Chinese tallow tree, red-leaf sweetgum, and red-leaf red maple, however, were highly similar (fig.27).

Reflectance Spectra Used for Calibration and Validation of Hyperion Reflectance Images

Non-Vegetated Reflectance Calibration and Validation Targets

Mean reflectance spectra obtained from measurements at seven oil platforms exhibited similar shapes but high spectral variability (fig. 28). Not only did spectral magnitudes vary highly from site to site, but also the spectra of about half the calibration target sites exhibited fairly high internal variance, thus indicating that spectrally variable materials comprised the oil platform surface. Because of the significant variance from site to site, reflectance results from the oil platform sites

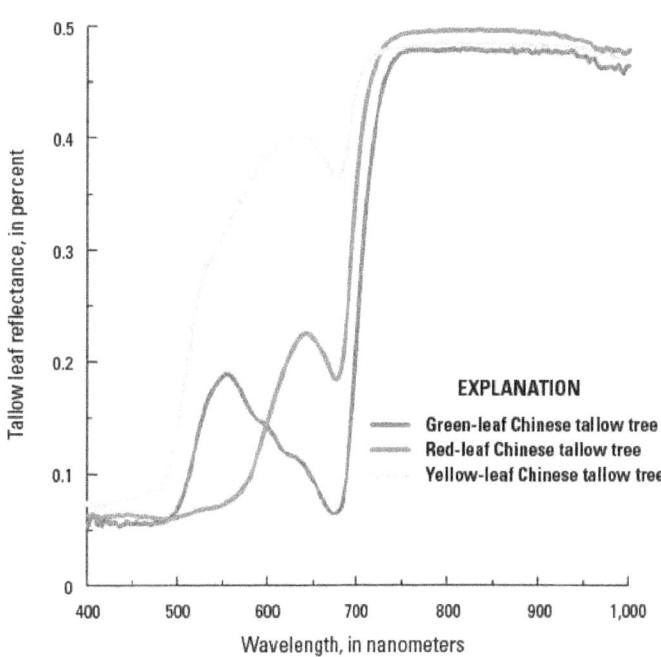

Figure 26. Representative reflectance spectra of green, red, and yellow Chinese tallow tree (*Triadica sebifera*) leaves collected in the Toledo Bend Reservoir study area.

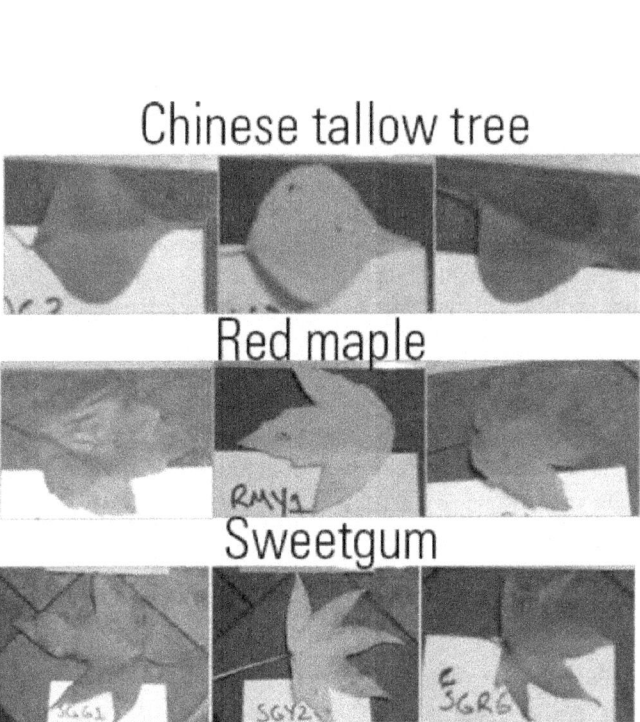

Figure 25. Leaf samples from Chinese tallow (*Triadica sebifera*), red maple (*Acer rubrum*), and sweetgum (*Liquidambar styraciflua*) trees in transition from live (green) to senescence.

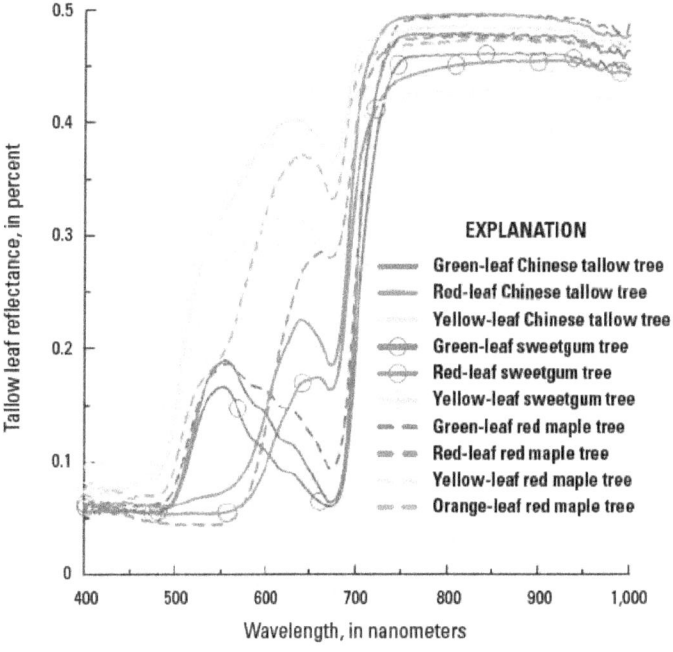

Figure 27. Representative reflectance spectra of green, red, and yellow leaves from Chinese tallow (*Triadica sebifera*) and sweetgum (*Liquidambar styraciflua*) *trees* and green, orange, red, and yellow leaves spectra from red maple (*Acer rubrum*) trees in the Toledo Bend Reservoir study area. Notice the high spectral overlap between leaves of the same color among the three species.

were not useful for calibration and validation of the calculated reflectance data obtained from the Hyperion sensor.

Vegetated Reflectance Calibration and Validation Targets

The helicopter-based collections of upwelling and simultaneous ground-based downwelling recordings for creation of canopy reflectance spectra of selected calibration and validation sites within the project area were undertaken on November 19, 2009. The vegetated sites consisted of young pine plantations, mature pine stands, grasslands, scrub-shrub stands, and hardwood and mixed forest stands each with and without Chinese tallow trees. Because of logistical problems, the helicopter carrying the radiometers to record the upwelling reflected sunlight from the target sites was launched late. The lateness of the launch and problems in platform stability severely limited the number and quality of canopy reflectance spectra obtained. Because of these limitations, the reflectance spectra calculated from the helicopter and simultaneous ground recordings were largely unusable for calibration of the atmospheric correction of the Hyperion data and validation of the Hyperion reflectance image products (following Ramsey and Nelson, 2005). Instead, ATCOR software was used to provide the necessary transformation of the Hyperion image data to canopy-reflectance estimates.

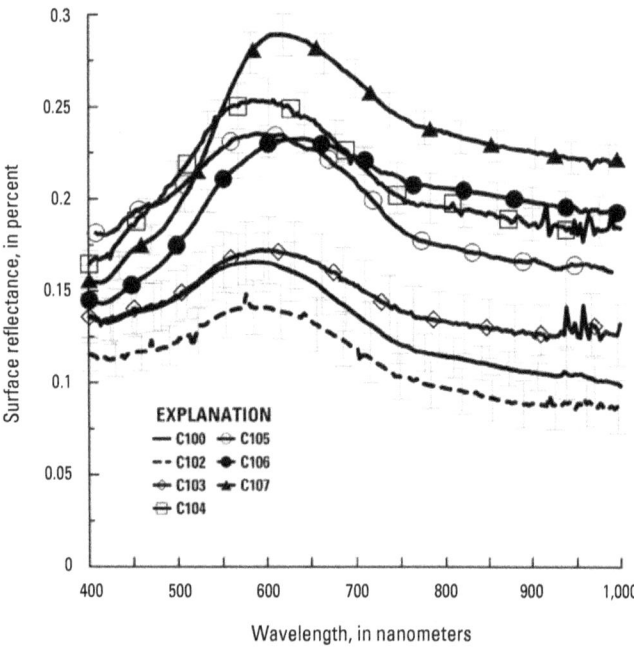

Figure 28. Mean reflectance spectra of the ground surface within oil-platform sites (C100–C107) in the Toledo Bend Reservoir study area. (See fig. 17 for locations and fig. 18 for fixed-wing photography of oil platforms at different stages of development.) Although the spectral variability about each spectrum characterizing the mean site reflectance was acceptable, the spectral variance between sites (amplitude differences among the reflectance spectra) was high.

Field-Based Landcover Classes and Features Associated with Chinese Tallow Tree and Red Trees

One objective of the ground and aerial surveys was to provide a spatial context for describing the occurrences of Chinese tallow trees within the Toledo Bend Reservoir study area. The most conducive description included associations by land class (comprising structure) and land features. In the end, the land classes and features found to best describe Chinese tallow tree occurrence closely duplicated (but without marshes) those used in the previous study of mapping Chinese tallow tree occurrences in southwestern Louisiana (Ramsey and others, 2005a). The land classes and feature classes distinguishable in the study area included the following: (1) pine forest; (2) hardwood forest; (3) mixed pine and hardwood forest; (4) planted pine (not including mature planted pine); (5) cypress forest (including all observed swamps); (6) scrublands (from clear-cut regrowth to dense mixtures of shrubs and trees of different varieties); (7) grassland (grazing and fallow fields); (8) bare surfaces that included mudflats, development, and clear cuts (associated with logging and containing minimal vegetation); (9) water (along lakes, ponds, or stream shorelines); (10) fence line; and (11) edge (an abrupt change in land class).

Observations of Chinese tallow trees during the ground surveys or red trees (including possible occurrences of Chinese tallow tree) during the fixed-wing aerial survey were associated with land classes and features that are described with accompanying photography (appendix 1). The organization of the photography emphasizes reoccurring classes and features in the landscape and how the Chinese tallow tree or red tree classes were associated with them. At most observation locations, multiple land classes and features were captured within the associated photography; however, the photograph titles define only the most meaningful single class or feature at each location. For instance, clear cuts, hardwoods, and planted pine classes may be all represented at a single location, but hardwood stands contained Chinese tallow trees or red trees. In that case, the class definition would be hardwood. For ease of reference, a separate map was created to show locations of all observations of Chinese tallow trees and red trees (including possible occurrences of Chinese tallow trees) during the fixed-wing aerial survey and ground-based reconnaissance (fig. 29).

Land Features

Chinese Tallow Trees on Edges

Although edges of landcover transition are not included in any land class, occurrences of Chinese tallow trees (or red trees in fixed-wing aerial reconnaissance) were often observed along such edges. During the ground and aerial surveys, occurrences were commonly observed in association with shrubs and trees in the subcanopy at the edge of forests adjacent to pine plantations, scrublands, roadways, clearings, and grasslands (fig. 30 *A–H*). As documented in the mapping of Chinese tallow tree occurrences in southwestern Louisiana, also observed during the current mapping project was that the abrupt edges were conducive to the establishment of Chinese tallow tree. Even though Chinese tallow or red tree sightings were more frequently observed on edges than other landscape features, sightings were still uncommon overall. Additionally, the Chinese tallow trees that were observed often retained a partial or full canopy of green leaves.

Chinese Tallow Tree at Water Edges

Chinese tallow trees occurred sporadically along ponds, streams, and the Toledo Bend Reservoir shoreline. Although they were found in locations adjacent to water, they most often occurred along obstructions near water bodies, such as a roadway guard rails, fences, or shrub lines. Although uncommon, as depicted in fig. 30*H*, Chinese tallow trees were at times even found in standing water.

Chinese Tallow Trees Along Fences

Chinese tallow trees and shrubs were most common along fence lines (fig. 31 *A–D*; but again, the qualification of "common" should be considered in the context of a generally uncommonly occurring feature).

Land Classes

Pine Plantations

In a previous project to map Chinese tallow tree, we found that shrub-pine plantations were susceptible to its establishment (Ramsey and others, 2005a). During the current mapping project, pine plantations were ubiquitous throughout the project area, as were clear-cut areas signifying ongoing silviculture (figs. 23F and 32*A, B*); however, in contrast to clear-cut areas, the pine plantation class varies widely in growth age and growth structure (or the patterns of canopy structure). It appeared that different methods were used to plant the pine seedlings, which resulted (with growth) in variable canopy structure patterns.

During the ground-based survey, we found that only one of the eight young plantation sites visited contained any Chinese tallow trees. During the fixed-wing aerial survey, red trees (including but not limited to Chinese tallow trees) were observed on 17 of 56 pine plantations, and these occurrences were for the most part located within nearby hardwood fingers protruding into the plantation. In contrast, two seemingly poorly managed pine plantations contained a fair amount of red trees, similar to occurrences documented in our previous mapping project for southwestern Louisiana (fig. 33*A, B*).

Mature Pine Forest

Mature pine forests included both nonplanted and planted pine forests (fig. 22*A–D*). The canopy structure or openness of the nonplanted and planted pine canopies appeared to differ, and as surmised in a previous Chinese tallow tree mapping project (Ramsey and others, 2005a), canopy gaps provide opportunities for Chinese tallow tree establishment. Even though distinction of nonplanted and planted mature pine stands was desirable, the spectral contrast between naturally occurring and planted mature pines was not distinct. As a result of their non-spectral separability, the nonplanted and planted mature pine forests were both included in the mature pine class. Of the forest classes, mature pine stands were associated with the highest frequency of documented observations of Chinese tallow trees during the ground survey and were also associated with one of highest observation rates of red trees (including Chinese tallow trees) during the fixed-wing aerial survey. Observations of red trees during the fixed-wing aerial survey were most often of understory red-leafed trees or shrubs that were observed from a nearly vertical orientation in relation to the target. As figures 22A and B suggest, however, opportunistic establishment within the gaps and open canopy of the mature pine forests is not limited to Chinese tallow trees. In addition, in instances where a pine forest abruptly adjoined a scrubland or pine plantation, red trees were at times observed at the forest edge during the fixed-wing aerial reconnaissance (figs. 30*A, B*).

Hardwood Forests

Hardwoods and bottomland hardwoods were combined into the same land class because these forests often contain similar associations of tree species. The difference in class designation represents a difference in inundation frequency and duration, but spectral distinction of the upland (hardwood) and wetland (bottomland hardwood) classes is often not possible.

Hardwood forests were associated with the second highest frequency (after pine forests) of Chinese tallow tree (ground survey) or red-tree (fixed-wing aerial survey) observations. As in pine forests, red trees in hardwood forests occurred most often in canopy gaps or where the canopy abutted a pine plantation, grassland, or scrubland (fig. 23D), and often only one or two red trees in the subcanopy were observed at any given location.

Hardwood Fingers

Although included in the hardwood forest land class, hardwood fingers were separately described because of their variable stand structure, particularly in relation to the length of exposed edges. During the fixed-wing aerial survey, red trees and shrubs were most often observed in the subcanopy of hardwood forests, particularly within narrow hardwood fingers. As illustrated in figure 23*A, B*, and *C*,

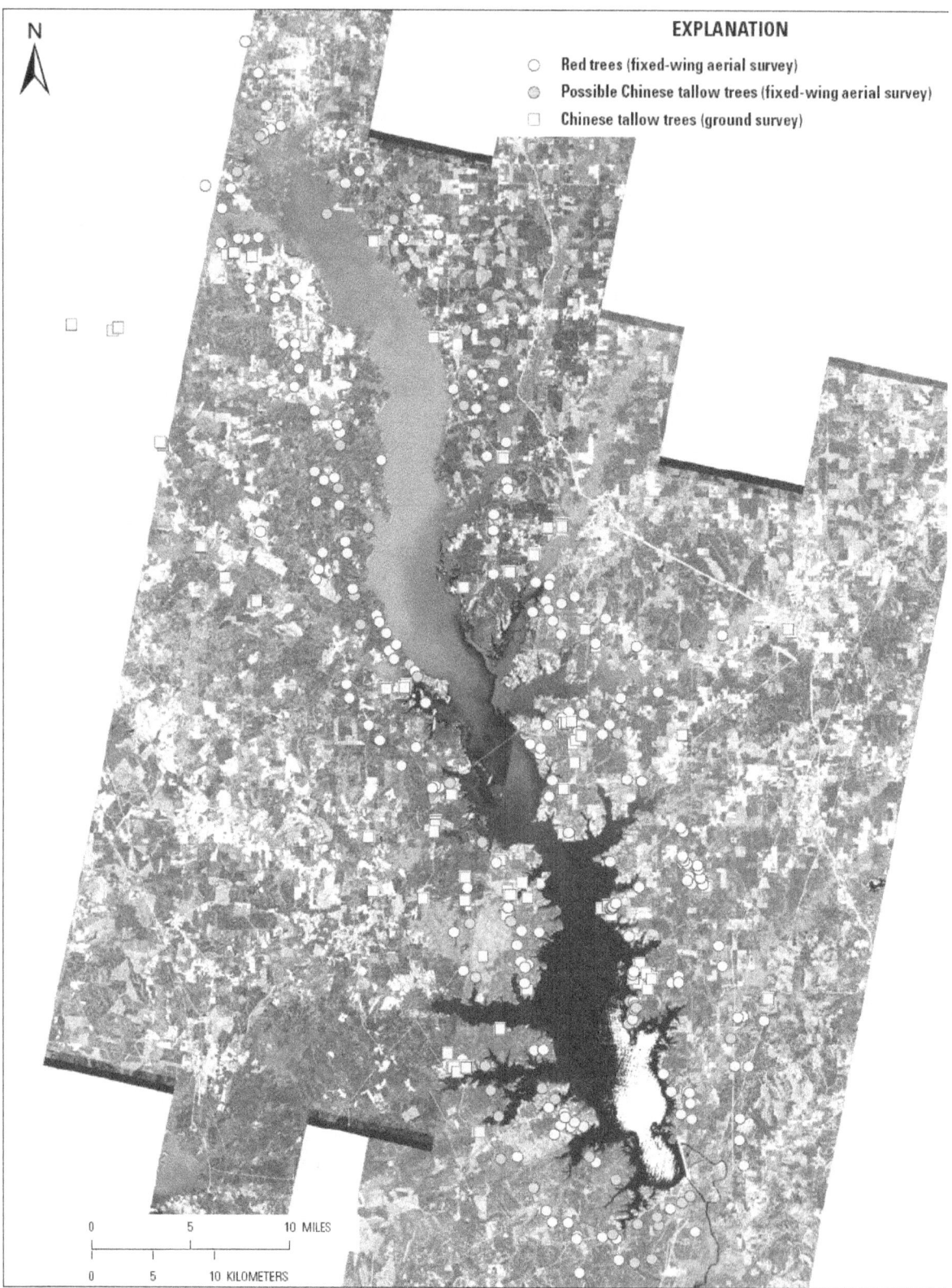

Figure 29. All field sites where Chinese tallow trees and red trees were observed during ground-based and fixed-wing aerial reconnaissance in the Toledo Bend Reservoir study area (Louisiana and Texas). For results of the aerial survey, a general category of "red trees" is used because red foliage of multiple trees and shrubs were indistinguishable. Where direct observations during the flight and (or) results of the ground survey indicated possible occurrences of Chinese tallow trees (within the red tree class), a category of "possible Chinese tallow tree occurrence" was introduced into the mapped results of the fixed-wing aerial survey.

Figure 30.   Chinese tallow trees (*Triadica sebifera*), or red trees and shrubs, observed during the ground survey, and red trees observed during the aerial survey in locations along forest edges. *A*, Red shrubs located along the edge of a young pine plantation. *B*, Scrubland in the understory of a mature pine forest. (Insets magnify the understory red shrubs.) A small patch of red shrubs located in the scrubland are pinpointed. *C, D*, Red- and green-leafed Chinese tallow trees along edges of fields. *E*, Green-leafed Chinese tallow tree shrubs along the edge of a power line clearing through a pine savannah. *F*, Red- and green-leafed Chinese tallow trees along a roadside. G, Chinese tallow tree shrubs along the edge of grasslands. *H*, Green-leafed Chinese tallow trees in a stream.

Figure 31.   Red- and green-leafed Chinese tallow trees and shrubs (*Triadica sebifera*) occurring along fences (A, B, C, D). The names on the photographs, for example, 2009_410M, indicate the site names, and more details of the sites can be obtained from the interactive query database available at the Web index page of this report.

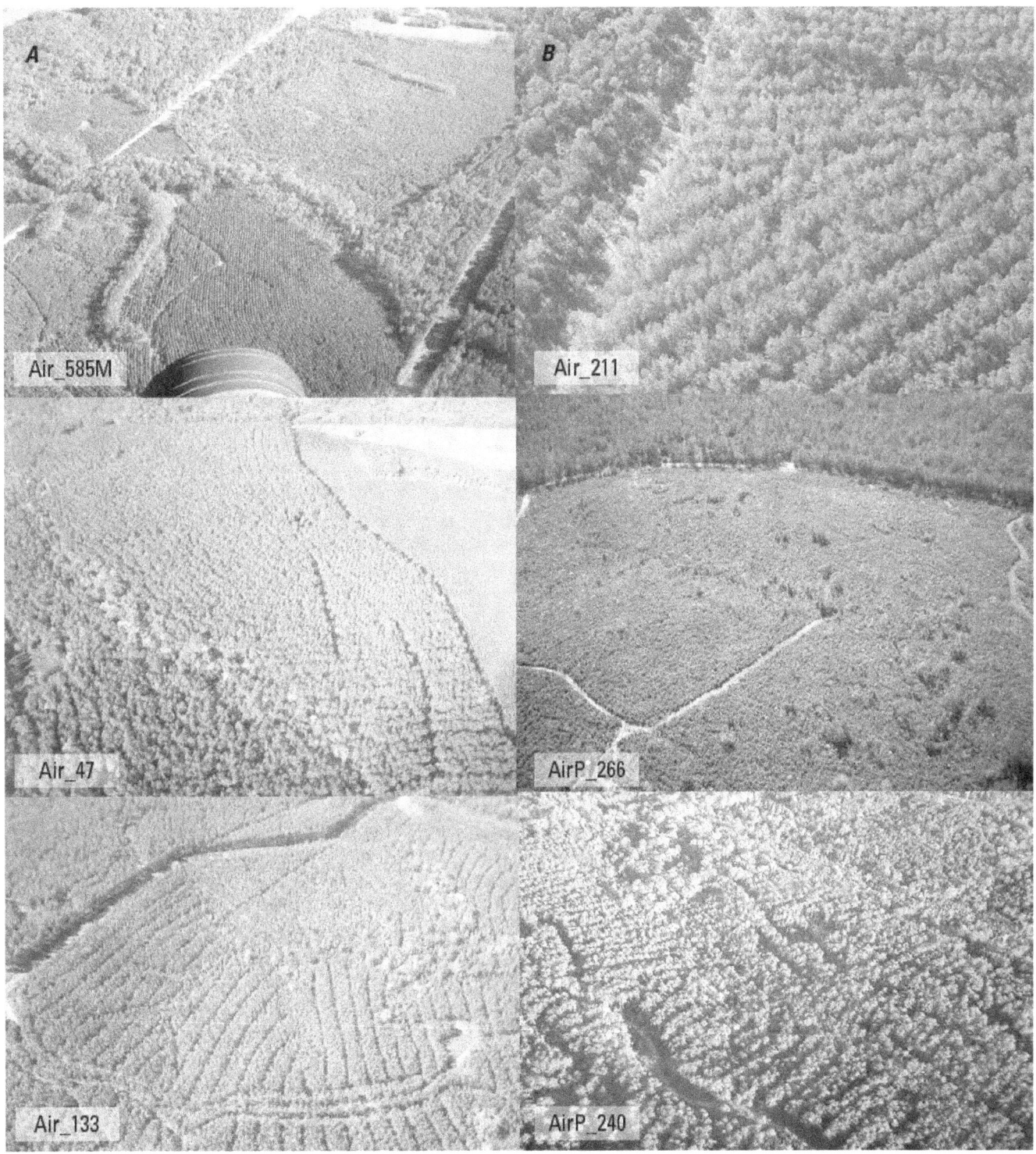

Figure 32. Pine plantations (*A, B*) at various stages of growth and with variable structural patterns were observed during the reconnaissance surveys. The interest in pine plantations was due to proclivity for establishment of Chinese tallow trees (*Triadica sebifera*) within this land class. In the Toledo Bend Reservoir project area, only minor occurrences of Chinese tallow trees were observed, even in the nonreplanted clear cuts. In at least two cases, however, the establishment pattern of Chinese tallow trees imitated that observed in pine plantations of southwestern Louisiana (fig. 33 *B*). These occurrences appeared where maintenance of the planted pine appeared to be lacking. The names on the photographs, for example, Air_585M, indicate the site names, and more details of the sites can be obtained from the interactive query database available at the Web index page of this report.

Figure 33. Red-leaf Chinese tallow trees (*Triadica sebifera*) occurring in pine plantations. *A,* Photograph taken during the helicopter aerial survey. *B,* Photograph taken during the fixed-wing aerial survey.

hardwood fingers penetrating into regrowing clear-cut areas or scrublands or into pine plantations provided an even higher percentage of forest to shrub edges in relation to stand area (fig. 30*A*). Although not a statistical survey, in our aerial observations, only scrublands were associated with a higher occurrence of red trees than were hardwood fingers. This same association was not prevalent where hardwood fingers were interlaced within mature pine forests (fig. 23*E* and *F*). In these cases, red trees were not often detected, possibly because they were hidden by the dense overstory canopy or because they had not become established because there was lack of abrupt structural forest edge.

Pine and Hardwood Mixed Forests

Pine and hardwood species were often mixed into a composite forest structure. The association of red trees (detected during fixed-wing aerial survey) within these mixed forests followed the same pattern as in the pine or hardwood forests.

Grasslands

For the most part, the grassland class comprised agricultural fields used for grazing or fallow fields. Although fairly ubiquitous throughout the study area, grasslands did not normally dominate the landscape. In all fixed-wing aerial observations of grassland classes, there were no observations of red trees (including Chinese tallow trees) (fig. 34*A, B*). During the ground-based survey, however, grasslands

containing clumps of trees and shrubs were some of the most likely places to find Chinese tallow trees (fig. 34*C–H*). By far, the highest density of shrub-sized Chinese tallow trees was observed in a field that looked as though it had been fallow for some time (fig. 34*H*). Even this relatively dense population was fairly scattered and unremarkable except when compared to the general lack of Chinese tallow trees elsewhere in the study area. In addition, as depicted in figs. 34*C, D,* and *E* and common to a majority of Chinese tallow tree sightings, a good portion, if not the dominant portion, of Chinese tallow tree leaves had not turned red and remained mostly or totally green. Although relatively more common in the grassland class than all other land classes except possibly scrublands, Chinese tallow tree occurrences were uncommon in grasslands within the Toledo Bend Reservoir study area, and those occurrences tended to be a few shrubs or isolated trees that exhibited a high proportion of green leaves.

Scrublands

Scrublands were the most likely land class to contain Chinese tallow tree. As illustrated in the fixed-wing aerial survey (fig. 35*A–D*), however, red trees (including possible occurrences of Chinese tallow trees) in scrublands were still highly scattered and were not often observed. When Chinese tallow tree shrubs were observed during ground surveys, the leaves were as likely or more likely to be green instead of red (figs. 35*E–H*). Based on ground and aerial observations, however, scrubland was a minor land class and largely

Figure 34.   Photographs of grassland areas within the Toledo Bend Reservoir study area (Louisiana and Texas). *A, B,* Aerial photographs of large fields devoid of red-leaf Chinese tallow trees (*Triadica sebifera*). *C, D,* and *E,* Ground photographs of green- and red-leaf Chinese tallow trees and shrubs. *F, G,* and *H,* Ground photographs of red-leaf Chinese tallow tree shrubs. In *F,* the arrow differentiates the red-leaf Chinese tallow tree shrub from the red sumac shrub next to it in the foreground. In *H,* the most dense occurrence of red-leaf Chinese tallow trees and shrubs observed in all reconnaissance surveys is shown.

consisted of shrubs and grasses in clear-cut areas not yet replanted and in somewhat small, scattered patches.

Cypress Forests

Although a minor land class in the project area, cypress forests occupy a unique position in the project landscape (fig. 36). Cypress forests are included in the broad wetland forest class, as are bottomland hardwood forests. Compared to upland forests, both bottomland hardwood and cypress forests undergo more frequent and longer inundations; however, bottomland hardwood inundations are infrequent compared to the permanent to semipermanent inundations of cypress forests. Even though flooding is nearly permanent in cypress forests, Chinese tallow trees can become established in these unique forests (Ramsey and others, 2005a). Spectral distinction and classification of cypress forests within the Toledo Bend Reservoir study area relied on relatively low stand density and the presence of saturated soils or standing water backgrounds. Chinese tallow trees were not observed in any cypress forests during the fixed-wing aerial survey.

Bare/Developed

The most important landcover subclass included in the bare/developed class was clear-cut land (figs. 37–38). Widespread clear cutting that had occurred and was occurring within the forested areas dominated the more dramatic and frequent spatial changes in the vegetated landscape. The clear cuts existed in a variety of structural forms. These forms included replanted clear cuts ranging from newly planted pine seedlings (exhibiting wide, mostly bare spaces) to mature pine regrowth (exhibiting dense stands). Others were freshly cleared with residual woody material still covering the clearing, while older clearings had been cleared without replanting. Most often, these latter areas contained grasses and shrubs.

Bare and un-replanted surfaces formed by clear cutting can form environments conducive for Chinese tallow tree establishment. Spectral distinction between bare ground, paved surfaces, and other largely nonvegetated surfaces was not directly possible, but distinction of these classes can be improved through the application of spatial association information (Ramsey and others, 2001). For this study, however, nonvegetated surfaces were not of immediate importance in detecting Chinese tallow trees. Further classification processing to distinctly identify clear-cut land classes was not performed.

Interactive Query of Reconnaissance Site Information

An interactive query system was implemented to combine the reconnaissance information contained in the site summary catalogue (appendix 1) with a map containing all aerial (fixed-wing aircraft and helicopter) and ground-site locations (fig. 39

and downloadable database from the Web index page of this report) overlaid on 2010 DOQQs of Louisiana and Texas. In addition to information displayed interactively, the database contains a landcover class variable and a notation stating the presence or absence of Chinese tallow trees or red trees at each site. The Chinese tallow tree variable is only associated with ground- or helicopter-based observations. The red tree variable is only associated with the fixed-wing aerial observations. At sites observed from the fixed-wing aircraft, the "red tree" class included red maple, sweetgum, and red-leaf Chinese tallow trees or shrubs; it also possibly included poison sumac. Different symbols were used to identify each site with the date and type of reconnaissance activity.

Landcover Classification of Advanced Land Imager Data

The northern and southern ALI images were classified into six land classes and five water classes (fig. 40, table 7). The classification did not follow a particular national protocol but, rather, was based on visually distinct land classes observed during the ground and aerial surveys; they included planted pine, mature pine forests, hardwood forests, cypress forests, clear-cut scrub, grasslands, bare/developed, wetlands, and five water classes. The wetland class was defined based on the physical appearance of false-color composite photography and image data. The water classes mainly depict differences in water clarity or turbidity.

Pine Plantation and Mature Pine Forests

Collecting growth-stage information related to the canopy structure and age of pine plantations was an objective of the ALI landcover classification. Growth-stage information is important in identifying initial establishment of Chinese tallow tree; however, progressive stages in growth could not be captured because the differences amongst growth stages were not spectrally distinct (for example, Ramsey and others, 2005a and 2005b). To compensate for indistinct spectral boundaries, aggregation of the pine plantation classes into three growth stages—young pine plantation, shrub pine plantation (designating height), and mature pine plantation—was attempted. Even though mixing at the class boundaries was expected, the extensive confusion between the young and shrub pine plantation classes could not be overcome; therefore, they were combined into a single pine plantation class. Similarly, because of the high spectral confusion between mature pine plantations and "natural" pine forests, these two classes were combined as the mature pine forest class.

Hardwood Forests and Hardwood Fingers

The frequent observations during the ground and aerial surveys of hardwood fingers containing red trees and shrubs

Figure 35.   Photographs of scrubland areas within the Toledo Bend Reservoir study area (Louisiana and Texas). *A, B, C, D,* Regrowing clear-cut areas largely vacant of replanted pine. *D* includes a magnified inset depicting some red shrubs; however, the identity of the shrubs could not be determined from the photograph. *E, F, G, H,* Scattered red-leaf Chinese tallow trees (*Triadica sebifera*) in isolated and fairly small scrubland areas.

Figure 36. Aerial photograph of a cypress (*Cupressus L.* spp.) forest within the Toledo Bend Reservoir study area (Louisiana and Texas) acquired during the fixed-wing aerial survey.

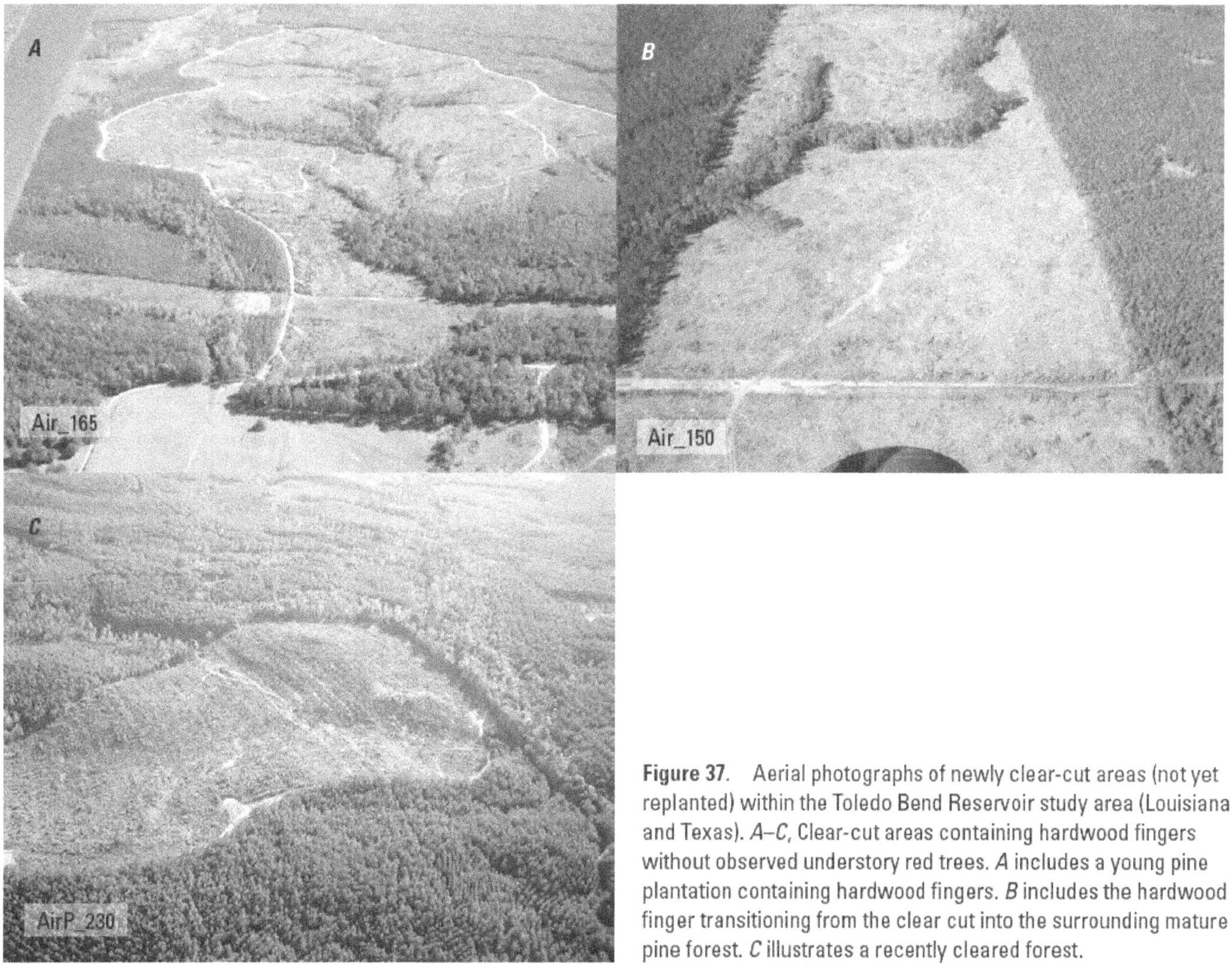

Figure 37. Aerial photographs of newly clear-cut areas (not yet replanted) within the Toledo Bend Reservoir study area (Louisiana and Texas). *A–C,* Clear-cut areas containing hardwood fingers without observed understory red trees. *A* includes a young pine plantation containing hardwood fingers. *B* includes the hardwood finger transitioning from the clear cut into the surrounding mature pine forest. *C* illustrates a recently cleared forest.

Figure 38. Photographs of developed areas containing red-leaf Chinese tallow tree (*Triadica sebifera*) within the Toledo Bend Reservoir study area (Louisiana and Texas). *A,* Service station. *B,* Private home.

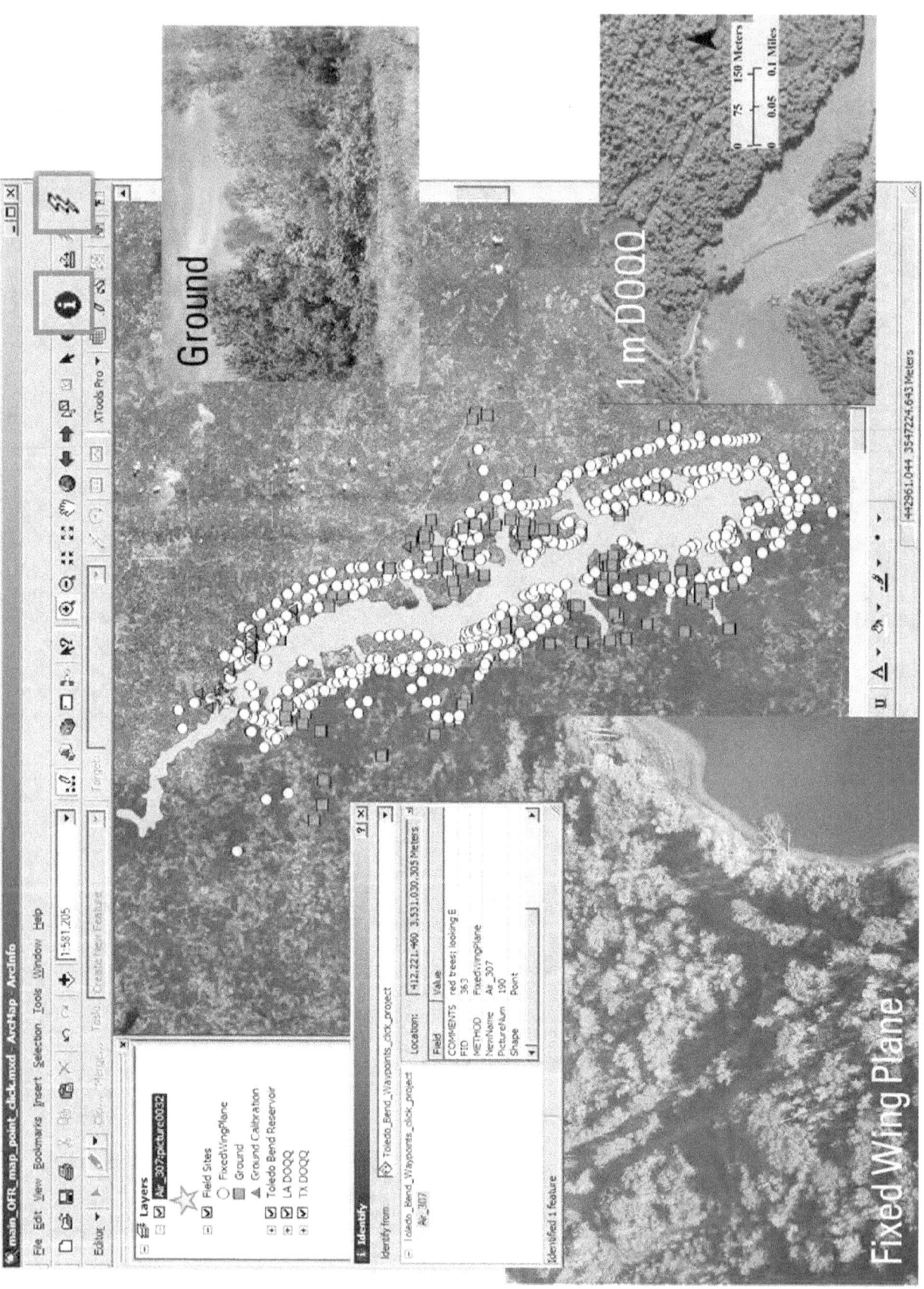

Figure 39. An example display of the interactive reconnaissance site database. The map user can select the identifier tool from the viewer main menu, then select one of the site locations (in this case "Air_307") to view attribute data, including field notes. For each site, there is also a regional view taken from the 1-meter (m) resolution, 2010 digital orthophoto quarter quadrangle (DOQQ). Photography obtained during the fixed-wing aerial survey is also available when selected by the user (via the "lightning bolt" hyperlink tool). The downloadable database is available from the Web index page of this report.

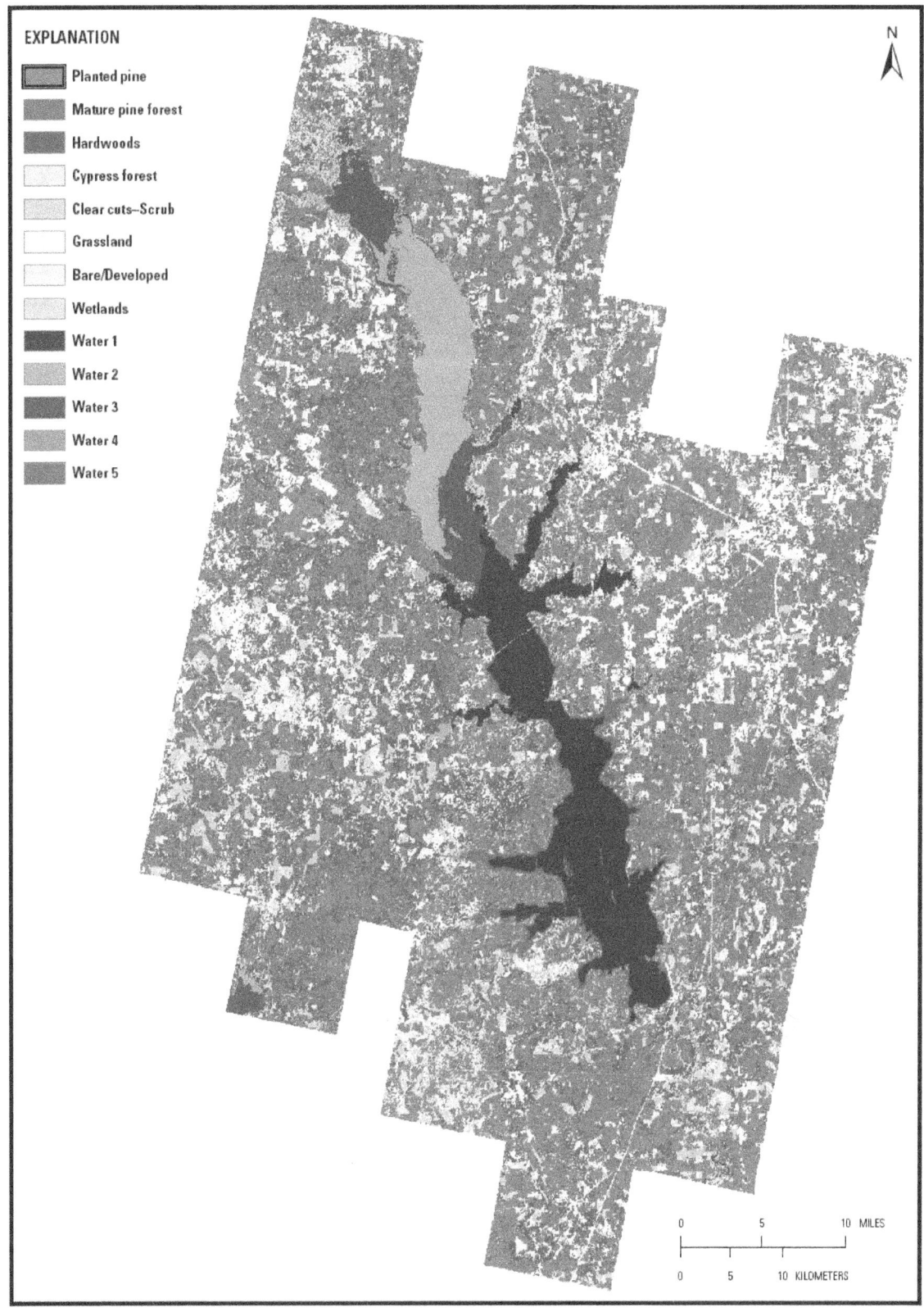

EXPLANATION

- Planted pine
- Mature pine forest
- Hardwoods
- Cypress forest
- Clear cuts–Scrub
- Grassland
- Bare/Developed
- Wetlands
- Water 1
- Water 2
- Water 3
- Water 4
- Water 5

Figure 40. Landcover map of the Toledo Bend Reservoir study area (Louisiana and Texas) based on data acquired by the Earth Observing-1 Advanced Land Imager sensor.

Table 7. Land classes identified within satellite imagery of the Toledo Bend Reservoir study area (Louisiana and Texas). Images were obtained by the Advanced Land Imager sensor aboard the Earth Observing-1 satellite.

[km², square kilometers]

Land Class	Total Area (km²)	Percent cover per Land class	Description
Planted Pine	1,471	28	Young planted pine
			Planted scrub pine
Mature Pine Forests	543	10	Mature planted and non-planted pine
Hardwoods Forests	1,310	25	Hardwoods and Bottomland Hardwoods
Cypress Forests	279	5	Cypress forest includes all observed swamp areas
Clear cuts-Scrubland	201	4	Regrowing clear cuts and scrublands
Grasslands	606	12	Grasslands including grazing lands and fallow fields
			Areas confused with scrub fields
Bare-Developed	147	3	Mudflats, developed (low intensity residential), roads and logged areas with minimal vegetation
Wetlands	66	1	Woody and emergent herbaceous
Water	293	12	Five different water types based on hue (most likely turbidity diffrences)
	151		
	115		
	34		
	45		

(including Chinese tallow trees) led us to attempt ALI-based mapping of hardwood forests, especially hardwood fingers, in the study area. As illustrated in fig. 23*E*, however, hardwood fingers were often nearly spectrally hidden within mature pine forests. In other cases, scattered or poorly defined hardwood stands were intermixed with shrubs and grasses (figs. 23*B* and 30*B*). Hardwoods were at times mistakenly classified as planted and mature pine forests and scrublands, particularly when the scrub shrubs or pines and hardwoods were intermixed (fig. 41). Mixed pixels within the ALI classification, such as those pixels that contained both the dirt road and the adjacent vegetation, often were misclassified as hardwoods. Prominently, these types of mixed pixels were misclassified within the hardwood-bottomland hardwood class throughout the project area, thus creating an overexpansive hardwood class.

Scrublands and Land Features

Scrublands were not distinguished in the landcover classification of the ALI imagery (fig. 35), so the amount of scrublands in the project area was not determined. In general, the scrubland class was mixed into the grassland, clear cut, and hardwood classes. The actual proportion of scrubland within each of the other land classes was not ascertained.

Land features, fences, and edges were not directly distinguishable in the ALI imagery; therefore, these classes were incorporated into the surrounding land classes. For instance, fences were most often included in the surrounding grassland class, and edges were included in pine plantation, pine, hardwood, and mixed forest classes.

Assessment of the Landcover Classification Map

A formal assessment of the classification accuracy was not conducted; however, the integrity of the classes as representing a particular land class was assessed by way of ground-based observations (including photography), aerial documentations, and the 2009 and 2010 DOQQ mosaics. At times, validation of class membership by using the DOQQs was hindered by the season when the DOQQ base photography was acquired. Photography collected late in the winter (late December to February) exhibited leaf-off conditions for most hardwoods and shrubs. In these cases, it was difficult to differentiate between types of hardwood forests, shrubs, and recently cleared lands. In addition to the difficulties related to leaf-off timing of photography, spectral confusion between land classes in the ALI images produced varying degrees of misclassification.

Based on the ALI landcover classification, the 5,261.9 km² landscape of the Toledo Bend Reservoir study area was dominated by pine and hardwood forests (covering around 35 percent) and pine plantations (covering 28 percent) (table 7). Grasslands (12 percent cover), primarily including grazing lands and fallow fields, existed, as did scrublands (4 percent cover) and cypress forests (5 percent cover) (table 7), but these land classes were relatively insignificant covers in the study area. Dominant landcover changes in the

Figure 41. Ground and aerial photographs of planted pine (*Pinus* L. spp.) areas in the Toledo Bend Reservoir study area (Louisiana and Texas). The locations of these areas are also illustrated on a 2010 digital orthophoto quarter quadrangle (DOQQ). Chinese tallow trees and shrubs are shown within a young pine plantation, and along the edges of a hardwood finger and the surrounding mature pine forest.

landscape were associated with forestry silviculture. In our previous study of southwestern Louisiana, Chinese tallow trees were found in cypress, hardwood, and pine forests and in pine and cypress plantations. Pine plantations, and some scrublands, contained some of the highest percent occurrences of Chinese tallow trees in the previous southwestern Louisiana study. Based on those previous findings, we expected similarly associated Chinese tallow tree occurrences.

Helicopter Reflectance Data Spectral Dataset

The lack of quality in the obtained helicopter-based canopy reflectance spectra was mainly related to the inability to consistently image the same location on the ground. This targeting inconsistency led to the result of there being a variable composition mixture in the canopy target, thus compromising the interpretability of the resultant canopy reflectance spectra in relation to canopy composition. Although the direct use of the spectra for creating a spectral indicator for red-leaf Chinese tallow tree was diminished, the canopy-reflectance spectra provided estimates of the magnitudes and variation associated with spectra of mature forests: planted pine and shrub canopies containing or not containing Chinese tallow tree.

An examination of the obtained spectra illustrates the nature of the composite canopy spectra, the reproducibility of the spectra, and the possible contrasts associated with contribution of red-leaf Chinese tallow trees to the canopy composition. In the first example, canopy spectra obtained from adjacent planted pine fields (one with and one without Chinese tallow shrubs) (fig. 24A) are nearly identical in the visible (VIS) (400–700 nm) range and only moderately differ in the near-infrared (NIR) (700–912 nm) wavelength region (fig. 42). Differences in NIR magnitude mainly pertain to contrasting amounts of live material in the radiometer IFOV, whereas, pertinent to this mapping, the contribution of red-leaf Chinese tallow tree is most often exhibited as comparatively higher red reflectance magnitudes (600–700 nm). The comparison of spectra from the adjacent pine plantations showed that the few red-leaf Chinese tallow tree shrubs amongst the planted pines were not reflected in the canopy spectra.

In a second example, the canopy spectrum of a mature pine forest is compared to the spectra of two young pine plantations (fig. 42). Higher red magnitudes would tend to indicate the presence of red-leaf Chinese tallow tree (or another red-leafed plant) within the pine forest composition; however, based on helicopter observations there was no Chinese tallow tree present at this site. In this case, the much lower NIR and somewhat higher red magnitudes of the pine forest spectra most likely reflect the high proportions of dead understory (visible in fig. 43), which contributes to the canopy composition within the radiometer FOV. Ideally, the combination of low NIR and somewhat higher red magnitudes would provide enough evidence to exclude red-leaf Chinese tallow trees as the cause of the increase in red reflectance and, instead, predict a higher proportion of dead material.

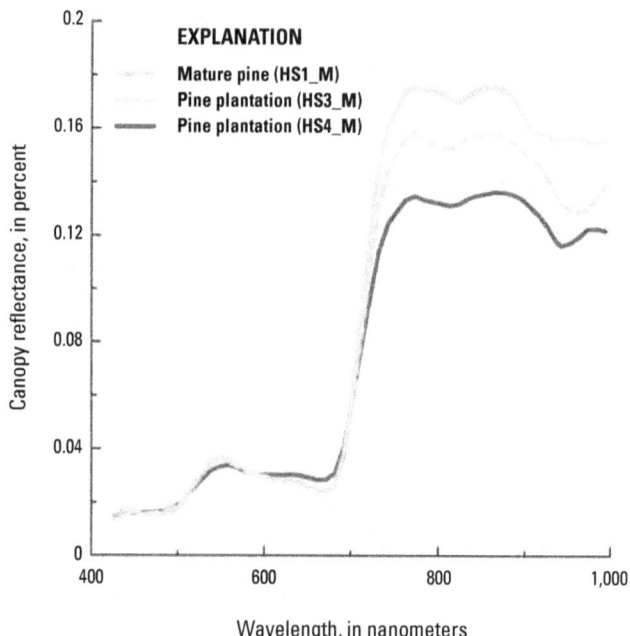

Figure 42. Canopy reflectance results for a mature pine (*Pinus* L. spp.) (HS1_M, also shown in fig. 43) and two young pine plantations within the Toledo Bend Reservoir study area (Louisiana and Texas [fig. 24A and fig. 41B]). The names, for example HS1_M, are the site names from where the spectra were collected.

Creating Indicator Spectra from the Helicopter Reflectance Spectral Dataset

PolyVector Analysis of Spectral Data

Even though uncertainty existed, the spectra were processed through the PVA suite of programs to ascertain whether or not a set of useable spectral indicators for Chinese tallow tree occurrences could be produced from helicopter-based spectra. By trial and error, mean-values of the helicopter-based canopy reflectance spectra obtained from the 12 calibration-validation sites were tested for consistency in results obtained via PVA. Five of the 12 canopy reflectance spectra were selected as the final PVA input dataset (fig. 44). The five helicopter-based spectra were associated with the following types of vegetation:

- One mature pine forest site,

- An isolated mixed pine and hardwood stand containing Chinese tallow tree,

- Two pine plantation sites (one containing a few Chinese tallow shrubs),

- One scrub-shrub site containing Chinese tallow tree, and

- Senescent vegetation spectra obtained from the 2002 Chinese tallow tree study in southwestern Louisiana (Ramsey and others 2005a).

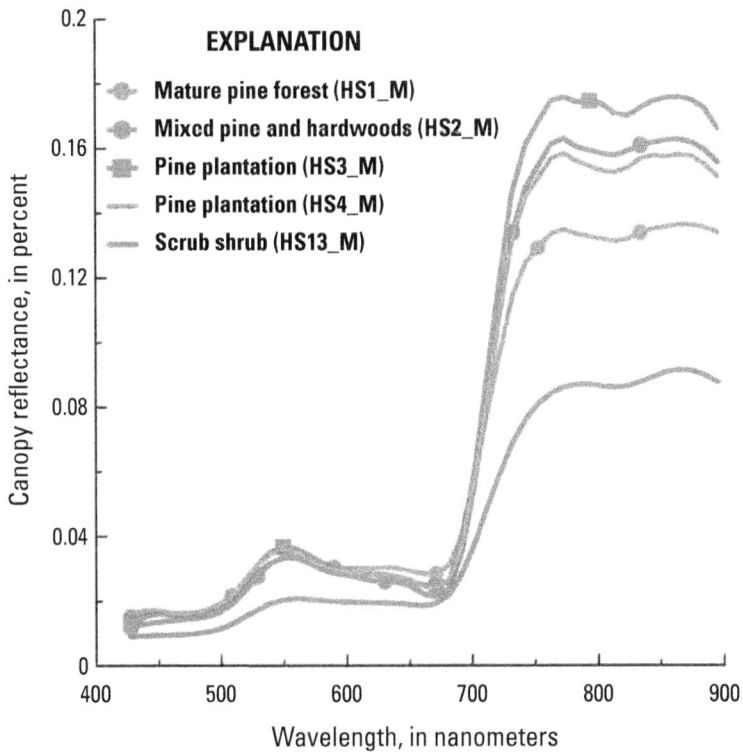

Figure 43. Aerial photograph of a mature pine (*Pinus* L. spp.) stand in the Toledo Bend Reservoir study area (Louisiana and Texas). As the illustration shows, the stand contained high proportions of senescent grass understory.

EXPLANATION

- Mature pine forest (HS1_M)
- Mixed pine and hardwoods (HS2_M)
- Pine plantation (HS3_M)
- Pine plantation (HS4_M)
- Scrub shrub (HS13_M)

Figure 44. Canopy reflectance spectra based on helicopter upwelling sunlight recording of four pine (*Pinus* L. spp.) forests and plantations and one scrub-shrub site within the Toledo Bend Reservoir study area (Louisiana and Texas). These spectra were selected for processing by PolyVector Analysis in order to determine indicator spectra for Chinese tallow tree (*Triadica sebifera*). The names, for example HS1_M, are the site names from where the spectra were collected.

These indicator spectra did not define the components of a typical canopy as green, red, and brown (or nonliving) materials but, rather, as the integrated composite of the canopy materials, one of which contained some proportion of red-leaf Chinese tallow trees (fig. 45, table 8). Although we were not able to derive a unique indicator spectrum for red-leaf Chinese tallow trees from the helicopter-derived canopy reflectance spectra, the composition spectra provided at least an initial set of indicator spectra for possibly detecting vegetation represented within the Hyperion image that was associated with a higher relative likelihood of containing Chinese tallow trees or red trees. These indicator spectra were subsequently combined into canopy reflectance spectra datasets extracted from the Hyperion reflectance images in order to promote the detection of Chinese tallow trees or at least provide locations of higher likelihood of occurrences.

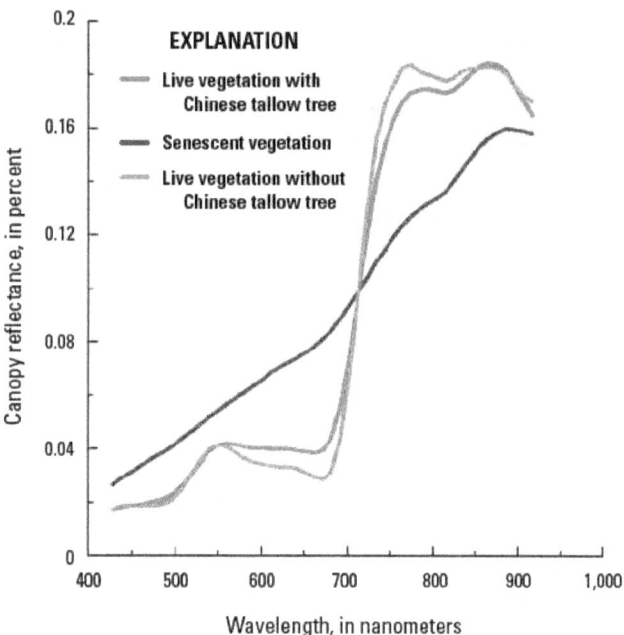

Figure 45. Canopy reflectance of three indicator spectra used for detecting Chinese tallow tree (*Triadica sebifera*) occurrences within the Toledo Bend Reservoir study area (Louisiana and Texas). The variance of the five reflectance spectra were adequately described by three indicator spectra: the first represents live vegetation (pine) without Chinese tallow tree, the second represents senescent vegetation, and the last live vegetation (pine and mixed hardwoods) with Chinese tallow tree. The correlation strength among the three indicator spectra and the five input spectra is provided in table 8. The indicator spectra shown in figure 45 are identified by a row of ones and zeros in table 8. The indicator spectra were derived from a PolyVector Analysis of variance among five input spectra (fig. 44).

Table 8. Results of PolyVector Analysis of spectra obtained during helicopter reconnaissance for Chinese tallow tree (*Triadica sebifera*) in the Toledo Bend Reservoir study area (Louisiana and Texas). Analysis of the five input spectra resulted in three indicator spectra representing live vegetation (pine) without Chinese tallow, senescent vegetation, and live vegetation (pine and hardwoods) with Chinese tallow (red background), respectively. The entry in each cell provides the correlation magnitude between each vegetation type (row) in the input database and each indicator spectrum (column). The indicator spectra are identified by a column of ones and zeros.

Type of vegetation	Site	Field site	Indicator		
			1	2	3
Senescent vegetation	GR	Previous study	0	1	0
Mature pine forest	P14	HS1_M	0.95	0.19	0
Mixed pine and hardwoods	P25	HS2_M	0.69	0	0.48
Pine plantation	P35	HS3_M	0.78	0	0.37
Pine plantation	P4P	HS4_M	1	0	0
Scrub-shrub	P13	HS13_M	0	0	1

Percent Occurrences of Chinese Tallow Tree Indicated by Hyperion Reflectance Images

The PVA and subsequent SPUNMIX transformation of the Hyperion reflectance data to percent-occurrence values involved numerous trial and error experiments. As previously discussed, technical difficulties related to validation and calibration data limited full implementation of the successful strategy applied in southwestern Louisiana. Although this limitation affected our ability to interpret products produced by PVA and SPUNMIX, it did not directly affect the strategy used for mapping red-leaf Chinese tallow tree occurrences. To identify a red-leaf Chinese tallow tree spectral detection tool, we aggregated our PVA and SPUNMIX applications according to the content of the input databases. Each section describing the different input databases and resultant PVA and SPUNMIX performances represents multiple trial and error efforts, and representative illustrations are included where warranted.

PolyVector Analysis of Spectral Datasets

The first strategy we applied was successfully used in a previous project to map red-leaf Chinese tallow tree (by percent occurrence) in southwestern Louisiana. This strategy involved aggregating all major land classes into a single database for PVA processing. The constructed spectral datasets included average composite reflectance spectra extracted from pertinent Hyperion reflectance images. Locations for extraction of the average reflectance spectra were selected based on ground and air reconnaissance data pinpointing observations of Chinese tallow trees (during ground or helicopter surveys) or red trees (during the fixed-wing aerial survey). To these selected spectra, we added spectra for locations at which the presence or absence of Chinese tallow trees (or red trees) was unknown (lacking ground or aircraft observations). The database input to the PVA solely included composite spectra extracted directly from the Hyperion reflectance images.

The PVA resulted in suites of indicator spectra that faithfully represented the internal variance of the dataset, but no indicator spectra clearly reproduced the distribution of red-leaf Chinese tallow tree (or red tree) occurrences detected during the reconnaissance surveys. Even though noncongruence was high, PVA produced indicator spectra showing some promise for mapping Chinese tallow tree (or red tree) occurrences were reformatted (from the PVA output) and entered into the PCI SPUNMIX mapping procedure. Unfortunately, none of the occurrence images produced by the SPUNMIX procedure aligned with the observed and possible Chinese tallow tree occurrences documented during the ground and aerial (helicopter and fixed-wing aircraft) surveys. In contrast to reconnaissance observations, the Chinese tallow tree occurrences predicted by the SPUNMIX procedure were widely distributed and included many contiguous and extensive occurrences.

Seeding the PolyVector Analysis (PVA)

In an attempt to focus the PVA input database to a more desirable outcome, we seeded it with reflectance spectra known to be associated with red-leaf Chinese tallow tree. The known reflectance spectra were obtained from the following sources:

- Red-leaf Chinese tallow tree leaves (figs. 25 and 26),

- Red-leaf Chinese tallow tree indicator spectrum identified during a previous project to map Chinese tallow tree occurrences in southwestern Louisiana (Ramsey and others, 2005b),

- Adapted spectra of the Chinese tallow tree (red) leaf and of previously collected Chinese Tallow tree (red) canopy, and

- Indicator spectra produced from the helicopter-based canopy reflectance data (table 8, figs. 44 and 45).

Although seeding the PVA input database with known reflectance spectra somewhat improved on the results we obtained by solely using Hyperion reflectance spectra, the results still did not provide the detection capability we desired.

Seeding PolyVector Analysis (PVA) combined with Land Class Information

Our next step in trying to identify a well-conditioned Chinese tallow tree indicator spectrum by using PVA processing was to organize the PVA input database by land class. To develop a unique spectral identifier, we adapted and combined leaf and canopy spectra of red-leaf Chinese tallow trees. These indicator spectra were then seeded to the PVA input database and entered into the SPUNMIX procedure to produce occurrence maps. Along with the leaf-canopy indicator spectra, input to the SPUNMIX procedure also included spectra extracted from Hyperion imagery obtained at locations where red-leaf Chinese tallow trees (or red trees) were observed or not observed during ground and aerial surveys (table 9). The Hyperion imagery used was limited to the hardwood-bottomland hardwood land class within the 1D swath coverage on October 17 and November 11, 2009 (matching the ALI image data used in the landcover classification).

Mapping Chinese Tallow Tree Occurrences in the Hardwoods Class

PVA was applied to the (November 11, 2009) Hyperion reflectance spectra extracted from 12 unknown and 6 known sites (observed red trees) (see table 9) within the hardwood land class contained in the 1D swath (fig. 11). As was most often the case in our other analyses, one of the seed spectra contained in the dataset input into PVA was selected as the red-leaf Chinese tallow tree indicator spectrum (created Chinese tallow tree) (table 10, fig. 46). Correlations with the indicator spectrum exhibited proper magnitudes (1–5 percent), but four of the six sites where red-leaf Chinese tallow trees (or red trees) were observed during aerial reconnaissance had zero or negative associations (row entries under indicator 1) (table 10). The remaining two spectra, one selected by PVA from the unknown and the other from the observed sites, exhibited mixed results; however, this particular PVA (input of the leaf-canopy adapted spectrum and landcover spectra) produced the overall best results within these land-class associated spectral datasets, including seeded spectra. Based on the best possible criteria, this set of PVA-derived indicator spectra was entered into the SPUNMIX procedure, from which the red-leaf Chinese tallow tree percent-occurrence map for the hardwood landcover class was produced.

Limited to the Hyperion 1D swath coverage and the hardwood landcover class, SPUNMIX output percent occurrences that were associated with the red-leaf Chinese tallow tree indicator spectra (similar to those produced with PVA and included in table 10). Although SPUNMIX outputs 0 to 100 percent occurrences per pixel, for graphical clarity, the percent occurrences were transformed to a binomial variable that represents the predicted presence (1) or absence (0) of red-leaf Chinese tallow trees or red trees; no information is conveyed related to percent-occurrence magnitudes.

Table 9.   Database input to the PolyVector Analysis of preliminary indicator spectra created from leaf and canopy spectra and Hyperion reflectance spectra. The analysis was performed in an attempt to identify a unique set of spectral indicators for Chinese tallow tree (*Triadica sebifera*) in the Toledo Bend Reservoir study area (Louisiana and Texas).

[UTM15, Universal Transverse Mercator, zone 15; Air_*, fixed-wing plane survey field site]

	Site descriptor	Source	Locations
1	Created Chinese tallow tree indicator	Ground and helicopter	
2	hardwoodunknown1	Hyperion	434310E, 3510870N UTM15
3	hardwoodunknown2	Hyperion	432000E, 3503490N UTM15
4	hardwoodunknown3	Hyperion	436710E, 3500910N UTM15
5	hardwoodunknown4	Hyperion	431400E, 3498630N UTM15
6	hardwoodunknown5	Hyperion	435720E, 3492780N UTM15
7	hardwoodunknown6	Hyperion	434160E, 3483300N UTM15
8	hardwoodunknown7	Hyperion	428220E, 3474900N UTM15
9	hardwoodunknown8	Hyperion	429480E, 3463800N UTM15
10	hardwoodunknown9	Hyperion	427770E, 3457710N UTM15
11	hardwoodunknown10	Hyperion	427080E, 3452100N UTM15
12	hardwoodunknown11	Hyperion	418560E, 3440310N UTM15
13	hardwood-redtrees1	Hyperion	Air_208
14	hardwood-redtrees2	Hyperion	Air_225
15	hardwood-redtrees3	Hyperion	Air_225
16	hardwood-redtrees4	Hyperion	Air_227
17	hardwood-redtrees5	Hyperion	Air_384
18	hardwood-redtrees6	Hyperion	Air_234

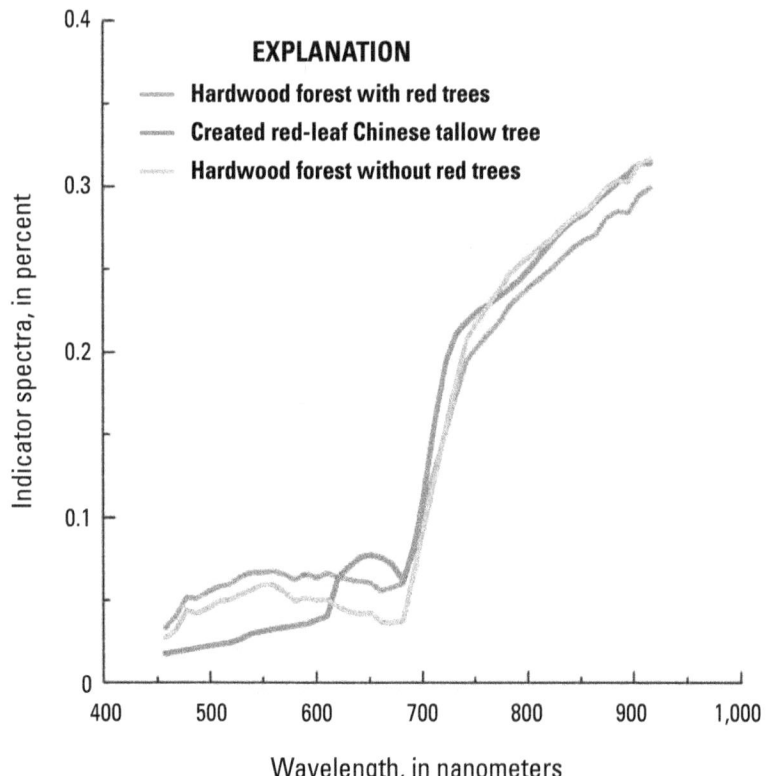

Figure 46.   Spectral results of a PolyVector Analysis of an input indicator spectrum for red-leaf Chinese tallow tree (*Triadica sebifera*) and Hyperion spectra from selected locations within the Toledo Bend Reservoir study area (Louisiana and Texas) (see table 9 input spectra). The resultant indicator spectra included the seed indicator spectrum for red-leaf Chinese tallow tree, a hardwood forest stand without red trees spectrum, and a hardwood forest stand with red trees spectrum.

Table 10. PolyVector Analysis output indicator spectra. Correlations of the three indicator spectra representing hardwood (with red trees), seeded indicator, and hardwood with all input spectra extracted from the Hyperion reflectance image within the hardwood landcover. The entry in each cell provides the correlation magnitude between each site descriptor (row) in the input database and each indicator spectra (column). The indicator spectra are identified by a column of ones and zeros.

[Air_*, fixed-wing plane survey field site; UTM15, Universal Transverse Mercator, zone 15. Red font signifies seed indicator spectrum, and green fonts denote indicator spectra associated with ground and aerial sites]

	Site descriptor[1]	Locations	Indicator		
			1	**2**	**3**
1	Created Chinese tallow tree indicator	Seed indicator	0.0000	1.0000	0.0000
2	hardwoodunknown1	434310E, 3510870N UTM15	0.3750	-0.0372	0.6621
3	hardwoodunknown2	432000E, 3503490N UTM15	0.5838	-0.0273	0.4435
4	hardwoodunknown3	436710E, 3500910N UTM15	0.4256	0.0263	0.5481
5	hardwoodunknown4	431400E, 3498630N UTM15	0.5546	0.0195	0.4259
6	hardwoodunknown5	435720E, 3492780N UTM15	0.7834	0.0261	0.1906
7	hardwoodunknown6	434160E, 3483300N UTM15	0.5793	-0.0501	0.4709
8	hardwoodunknown7	428220E, 3474900N UTM15	0.1602	0.0183	0.8215
9	hardwoodunknown8	429480E, 3463800N UTM15	0.5918	-0.0532	0.4614
10	hardwoodunknown9	427770E, 3457710N UTM15	0.7619	0.0128	0.2253
11	hardwoodunknown10	427080E, 3452100N UTM15	0.0000	0.0000	1.0000
12	hardwoodunknown11	418560E, 3440310N UTM15	0.5611	0.0104	0.4285
13	hardwood-redtrees1	Air_208	0.5902	0.0387	0.3711
14	hardwood-redtrees2	Air_225	0.7960	-0.0564	0.2604
15	hardwood-redtrees3	Air_225	0.5311	-0.0464	0.5153
16	hardwood-redtrees4	Air_227	0.6607	-0.0364	0.3757
17	hardwood-redtrees5	Air_384	1.0000	0.0000	0.0000
18	hardwood-redtrees6	Air_234	0.9336	0.0590	0.0075

[1]2–18 spectra extracted from Hyperion reflectance image.

The binomial overlay results were highlighted on two regions within the project area (fig. 47), one on the Louisiana side (fig. 48A) and the other on the Texas side (fig. 48B).

The overlay indicating expected Chinese tallow tree or red tree occurrences portrays a widely scattered distribution of Chinese tallow trees in the hardwood forests. As illustrated in figures 48A and 48B, fixed-wing observations of red trees do concur with the predicted occurrences; however, our reconnaissance data does not support the widespread establishment of Chinese tallow tree or red trees. For example, figure 48A contains insets showing the overlay and fixed-wing photography of the same area. In each of the three insets, although red trees are visible in the collocated photography, the predicted occurrences associated with senescing hardwoods are more extensive than were observed in ground and aerial reconnaissance. Of particular interest are the predicted occurrences shown in inset 3 of figure 48A associated similarly with senescent hardwoods; however, these hardwoods form hardwood fingers protruding into a young pine plantation. In this latter case, ground and aerial observations have confirmed relatively higher establishments of Chinese tallow trees or red trees.

Similar associations between predicted Chinese tallow tree or red tree occurrences and fixed-wing observations are shown in figure 48B. In inset 1 of figure 48B, scattered occurrences predicted within the hardwood forest and along the edges of isolated pine stands were not widely observed in the fixed-wing reconnaissance. Lack of confirmation, however, could be due to the difference in the times of the reconnaissance and image collection. In addition, Chinese tallow trees were observed in ground and aerial observations along edges, included along mature pine forests abutting pine plantations or shrubs. Similarly, inset 2 of figure 48B shows predicted occurrences within an area containing hardwood fingers and a young pine plantation, where yellow trees were observed and concentrated along edge, and within the hardwood fingers, where higher occurrences of Chinese tallow trees and red trees have been observed in ground and aerial reconnaissance. In this illustration, however, the predicted occurrences extend beyond the hardwoods, incorporating roadway and planted pines. This overextended prediction of Chinese tallow trees or red trees not associated with hardwoods is caused by the misclassification of hardwoods in the ALI imagery. Inset 3 of figure 48B exhibits the predicted

Figure 47.   Mapped occurrences of red-leaf trees. Indicator spectra output from PVA (fig. 46) were input into the SPUNMIX procedure that produced the occurrences of red-leaf Chinese tallow trees (*Triadica sebifera*) and red trees in association with hardwood forest stands and fingers within the Hyperion 1D swath coverage of the Toledo Bend Reservoir study area (Louisiana and Texas). The binomial representation of the SPUNMIX output is highlighted in figure 48 for insets "a" and "b."

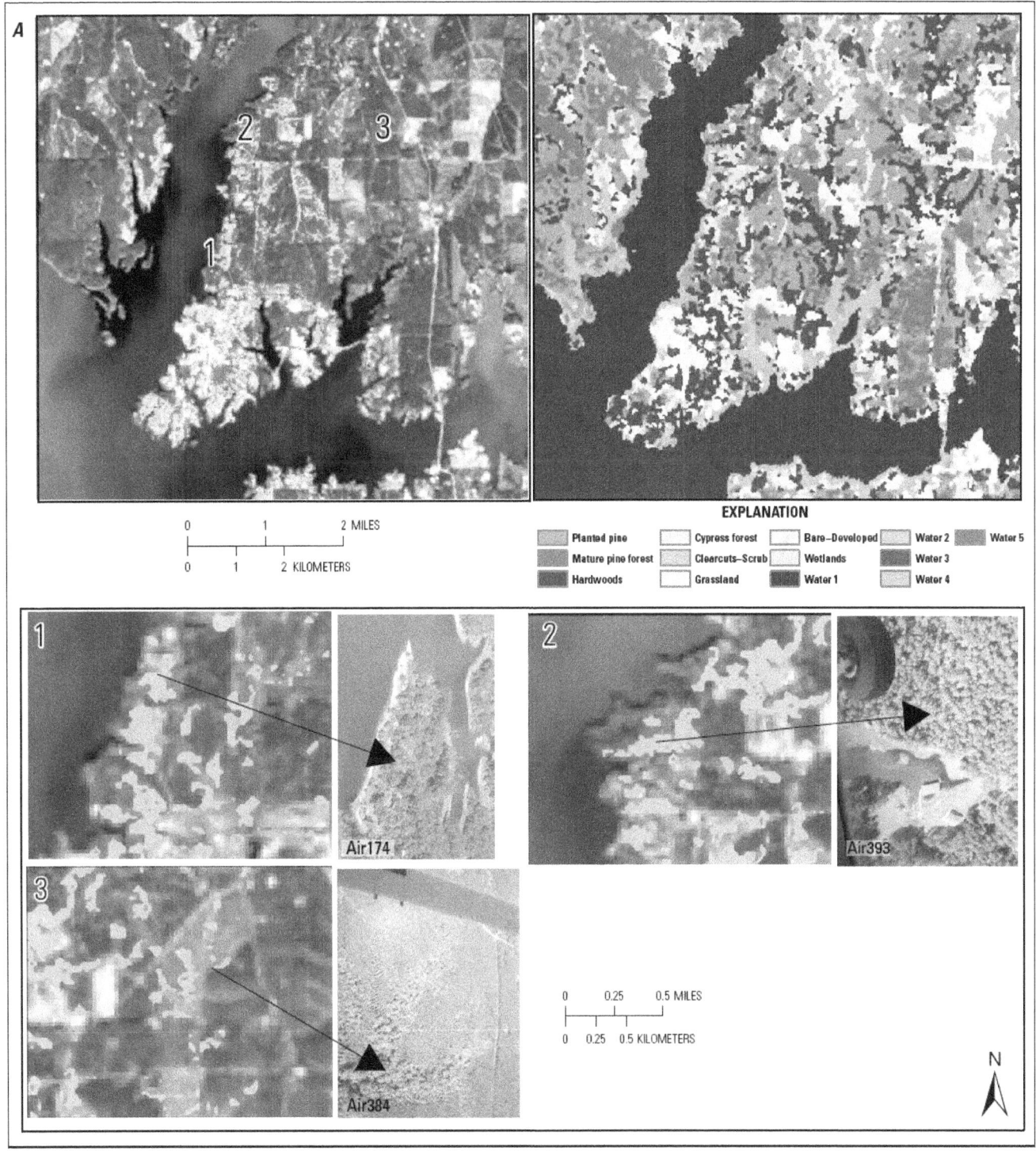

Figure 48A. A binomial representation of SPUNMIX-predicted occurrences (yellow mask overlay) of red-leaf Chinese tallow trees and red trees in association with hardwood forests and fingers in the Toledo Bend Reservoir study area (Louisiana and Texas). Areas of predicted occurrences are overlain on the mosaicked Advanced Land Imager coverages that were used in the landcover classification of the study area, and fixed-wing photos of the same areas are provided. *A,* Area corresponding to inset "a" on figure 47 (located on the eastern [Louisiana] side of the reservoir). Insets 1 and 2 illustrate occurrences within hardwood stands in pine forests, whereas inset 3 exhibits occurrences associated with hardwood fingers. The names on the photographs, for example Air49, indicate the site names.

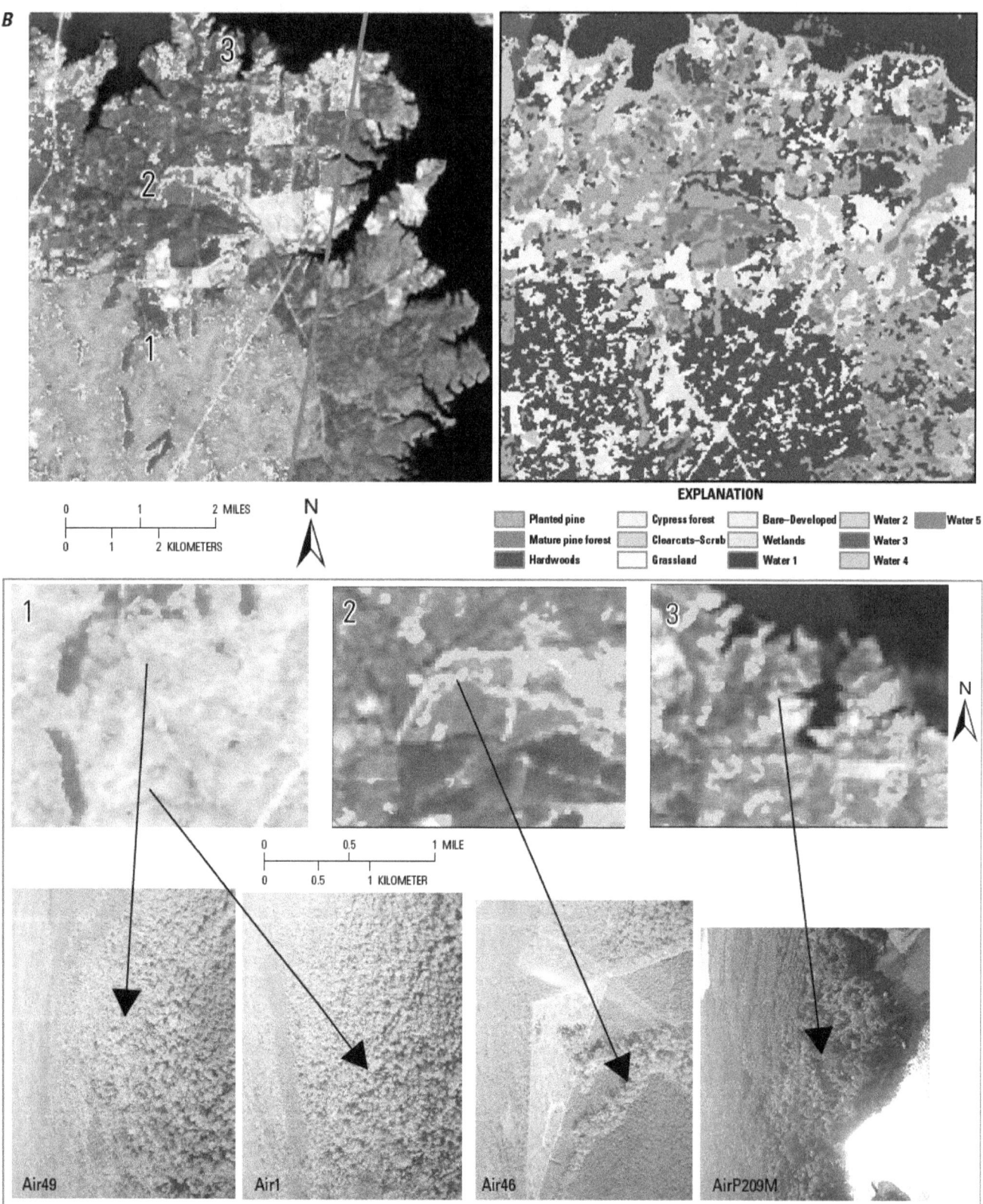

Figure 48B.   A binomial representation of SPUNMIX-predicted occurrences (yellow mask overlay) of red-leaf Chinese tallow trees and red trees in association with hardwood forests and fingers in the Toledo Bend Reservoir study area (Louisiana and Texas). Areas of predicted occurrences are overlain on the mosaicked Advanced Land Imager coverages that were used in the landcover classification of the study area, and fixed-wing photos of the same areas are provided. Area corresponding to inset "b" on figure 47 (located on the western [Texas] side of the reservoir). Inset 1 illustrates occurrences in a hardwood forest, inset 2 in an area of pine plantations, and inset 3 in hardwood stands in a pine forest. The names on the photographs, for example Air49, indicate the site names.

occurrences associated with senescing hardwoods. During fixed-wing aerial reconnaissance, red trees were observed at this location; however, as in all illustrations, the extensiveness of the predicted occurrences was not confirmed in the reconnaissance data.

Overall, the association of predicted distribution of Chinese tallow trees or red trees seems overemphasized. Although the predicted occurrences include observed red trees, they also extend into senescing hardwood-bottomland hardwood stands where red trees were not directly observed. In addition, erroneously predicted occurrences were associated with land classes other than hardwoods, but those artifacts were becuase of errors in the ALI landcover classification. Even accounting for prediction errors because of hardwood misclassifications, red-leaf Chinese tallow tree or red tree predicted occurrences seemed overextended into senescing hardwoods than reasonable. While observed Chinese tallow trees and red trees in hardwoods were correctly predicted by using the PVA seeded with the input indicator spectra shown in fig. 46, high errors of commission (inclusion of non-Chinese tallow trees and red trees) in the prediction seemed likely. In order to more fully assess this set of seed indicator spectra, we extended this occurrence mapping to other landcovers based on the same seed indicator spectra.

Extending the Seeded and *PolyVector Analysis (PVA)* to Multiple Landcover *Classes*

As in the PVA analyses of seeded spectral input data associated with the hardwood landcover class, PVA was applied to planted and mature pine, grassland, and hardwood associated spectral datasets extracted from October 17 and November 11, 2009, Hyperion reflectance images (1D swath). Spectral databases incorporating various seed combinations were input into the PVA analyses and results tracked and a summary of these attempts madc by using various datasets and combinations of seed spectra reported (table 11). Where the indicator associations (for example, numeric entries in table 11) indicated at least partial alignment with expectations based on the input known spectra, the resultant output indicator spectra were input into SPUNMIX and those results again tracked and noted in the last column of table 11.

No spectral seed combination, land cover class, or collection date produced a visually consistent landcover spatial distribution of Chinese tallow tree or red tree occurrences. As in the hardwood-associated mapping illustrated in figures 47, 48*A*, and 48*B*, errors in commission in the predicted occurrences often were judged too high. That failure lead to a simplified and generalized strategy focused on mapping higher likelihoods than directly detecting Chinese tallow tree occurrences. The likelihood mapping strategy entailed limiting the input seed spectra to those identified from the helicopter canopy reflectance dataset while retaining land class selectivity.

Seeding PolyVector Analysis (PVA) with Helicopter-Based Indicator Spectra in Hardwood Landcovers

The Hyperion-based reflectance spectra represented locations of observed (ground and aerial) and unknown occurrences of red-leaf Chinese tallow trees and red trees (fixed-wing aerial survey) in hardwood forests (table 12). The three helicopter-based seed spectra (see table 8, fig. 45) were included in the PVA input dataset (table 12). As described in the "Creating Indicator Spectra from the Helicopter Reflectance Spectral Dataset" section, new indicator spectra were calculated by PVA to represent the variance of the full input helicopter-based reflectance database. In this case, three indicator spectra that best represented the spectral variance of the input database were selected by PVA (fig. 49). The three indicator spectra included a Hyperion-based spectrum, "Indicator 1—live vegetation," representing an aerially observed location, and two helicopter-based PVA spectra, "Indicator 2—senescent vegetation" and "Indicator 3—live vegetation with red-leaf Chinese tallow tree."

Of the two helicopter-based indicator spectra, only Indicator 3 included a spectral response due to the occurrence of red-leaf Chinese tallow trees mixed into the live green vegetation canopy. The inability to discover a unique red-leaf Chinese tallow tree indicator spectrum as accomplished in Ramsey and others (2005a) meant that instead of mapping Chinese tallow trees directly, the likelihood of a canopy (within each pixel) to contain Chinese tallow trees or red trees was mapped. More specifically, the predicted occurrences referenced canopies that exhibited a spectral reflectance component with features similar to the mixed live vegetation and red-leaf Chinese tallow canopy indicator spectrum, thus indicating a higher likelihood of red-leaf Chinese tallow tree or red tree occurrence. The associations of these indicator spectra and all other input spectra (referring to locations in the Hyperion image) are provided in table 13.

The alignment of the input landcover spectra, the Hyperion-calculated indicator spectrum, and the two PVA-calculated indicactor spectra suggested that the ability to detect red trees or Chinese tallow trees within hardwood stands was intercorrelated with the performance of the seed live vegetation indicator spectrum. The helicopter-based seed live vegetation indicator spectrum (row 3 and column 3 of table 13) exhibited a high correlation (77 percent, column 3) with the helicopter-based seed live vegetation with Chinese tallow indicator spectrum. Indicator 3 reflecting correlations with the live vegetation with Chinese tallow tree seed-indicator was also associated highly (9 and 18 percent) with a locations containing higher observed concentrations of observed Chinese tallow trees along a fence line and along a forest edge (rows 7 and 11 of table 13). Remaining correlations with Indicator 3 within hardwood stands containing observed red trees or Chinese tallow trees were varied and low. Magnitudes of correlation between Indicator 3

Table 11. Summary of mapping results achieved by using various datasets and combinations of seed spectra aimed at producing a unique set of indicator spectra for detecting red-leaf Chinese tallow tree (*Triadica sebifera*) occurrences in the Toledo Bend Reservoir study area (Louisiana and Texas).

[No., number; PVA, PolyVector Analysis; em, endmember indicator; TBRT, tallow leaf bright; TC, tallow canopy; TCMED, tallow canopy and leaf medium; TDRK, tallow leaf dark; TLF, tallow leaf; TMED, tallow leaf medium]

Land class	Hyperion image swath and date	No. of training spectra from Hyperion image for PVA	Seeding with ground, canopy and created indicator spectra	PVA-output em	Analysis–Results	PVA indicator spectra used in spectral unmixing of Hyperion image (46 bands) to create percent occurrence maps
					Class stratified seeded	
Pine planted	ID -11Nov 2009	10	2002 tallow canopy and helicopter '09 (green vegetation)	none	no good indicator for tallow discrimnation	
		10	i)2002 TC and non-live material	none	no good indicator for tallow discrimnation	
			ii) TBRT			
			iii) TMED			
			iv) TDRK			
			v) TLF			
		13	two helicopter '09 spectra (green vegetation and green with red)			
			i) TLF	i) none	i)no good indicator for tallow	
			ii) TC	ii) 3em fuzzy	ii)no good indicator for tallow	
			iii) created TCMED	iii) 3em fuzzy weighted more on slightly on helicopter seeds	iii) maybe tallow indicator	iii) and iv) percent occurrence map did not show presence of tallow where observed on ground
			iv) created TCMED2	iv) 3em fuzzy weighted more on slightly on the helicopter seeds	iv) maybe tallow indicator	

Table 11. Summary of mapping results achieved by using various datasets and combinations of seed spectra aimed at producing a unique set of indicator spectra for detecting red-leaf Chinese tallow tree (*Triadica sebifera*) occurrences in the Toledo Bend Reservoir study area (Louisiana and Texas).—Continued

[No., number; PVA, PolyVector Analysis; em, endmember indicator; TBRT, tallow leaf bright; TC, tallow canopy; TCMED, tallow canopy and leaf medium; TDRK, tallow leaf dark; TLF, tallow leaf; TMED, tallow leaf medium]

			Class stratified seeded			
Land class	**Hyperion image swath and date**	**No. of training spectra from Hyperion image for PVA**	**Seeding with ground, canopy and created indicator spectra**	**PVA-output em**	**Analysis–Results**	**PVA indicator spectra used in spectral unmixing of Hyperion image (46 bands) to create percent occurrence maps**
Hardwoods	ID -11Nov 2009	11	i) Air_208	i) 3em weighted more on on Air_208	i) maybe red tree indicator	i) gave percent occurrence of red trees map did not correspond with observed field points
			ii) Air_208 and tallow canopy	ii) 3em	ii) no red tree discrimnator	
		11	Air_208, Air_225, Air_234, 2009_384 and			
			i) created TCMED2	i) 3em weighted more on on ground and air points showing red trees	i) maybe a red tree indicator	i) gave percent occurrence of red trees but it did not correspond with observed field points
			ii) adapted TCMED3	ii) 3 em	ii) no good red tree indicator	
			iii) TLF	iii) 3 em	iii) no good red tree indicator	
		19	1) Air_208, Air_225, Air_234, 2009_384	1) none	1) no red tree indicator	
			2) Air_208, Air_225, Air_234, 2009_384 and			
			i) created TCMED	i) none	i) no red tree indicator	
			ii) created TCMED2	2ii) em3 is weighted more on Air point with red trees	2ii) maybe a red tree indicator	2ii) did not give percent occurrence of red trees
			iii) created TCMED3	2iii to 2 vi – none	2iii) to 2vi) no red tree indicator	
			iv) TBRT			
			v) TDRK			
			vi) tallow canopy			

Table 11. Summary of mapping results achieved by using various datasets and combinations of seed spectra aimed at producing a unique set of indicator spectra for detecting red-leaf Chinese tallow tree (*Triadica sebifera*) occurrences in the Toledo Bend Reservoir study area (Louisiana and Texas).—Continued

[No., number; PVA, PolyVector Analysis; em, endmember indicator; TBRT, tallow leaf bright; TC, tallow canopy; TCMED, tallow canopy and leaf medium; TDRK, tallow leaf dark; TLF, tallow leaf; TMED, tallow leaf medium]

Land class	Hyperion image swath and date	No. of training spectra from Hyperion image for PVA	Seeding with ground, canopy and created indicator spectra	PVA-output em	Analysis–Results	PVA indicator spectra used in spectral unmixing of Hyperion image (46 bands) to create percent occurrence maps
				Class stratified seeded		
Grasslands	ID -11Nov 2009	14	1)2009_410,2009_415,2009_421,2009_504,2009_505 and			
			i) tallow leaf	i) 3em	i) 3em gives some solution	i) gave percent occurrence of red trees but did not correspond with observed field points
			ii) tallow canopy	ii) 3em	ii) 3em gives a better solution for red tree indicator	ii) gave percent occurrence of red trees but did not correspond with observed field points
			iii) tallow leaf bright red	iii) none	iii) has no solution	
			iv) tallow leaf medium	iv) 3em	iv) 3em maybe a red tree indicator	iv) did not give percent occurrence of red trees
		18	1)2009_410,2009_415,2009_421,2009_504,2009_505, Air_578 and			
			i) created tallow indicator3	i) 3em	i) maybe a red tree indicator	i) to iii) percent occurrence maps did not show any correspondence with ground observations
			ii) created tallow indicator1	ii) 4em	ii) maybe a red tree indicator	
			iii) tallow leaf bright	iii) 4em	iii) some indication	
			iv) tallow canopy	iv) 4em	iv) maybe a talllow indicator	iv) the percent occurrence map had some correspondence with ground observations
Mature Pine		25	i) tallow canopy	i) none	no good indicator for tallow discrimnation	
			ii) tallow leaf and green helicopter spectra	ii) none		
			iii) tallow leaf medium	iii) none		
		32	i) tallow leaf bright	i) none		
			ii) tallow leaf medium	ii) none		
			iii) tallow canopy	iii) 6em	iii) may give a tallow indicator	iii) did not give percent occurrence of red trees
			iv) created tallow canopy and leaf medium (TCMED)	iv) none		

Table 11. Summary of mapping results achieved by using various datasets and combinations of seed spectra aimed at producing a unique set of indicator spectra for detecting red-leaf Chinese tallow tree (*Triadica sebifera*) occurrences in the Toledo Bend Reservoir study area (Louisiana and Texas).—Continued

[No., number; PVA, PolyVector Analysis; em, endmember indicator; TBRT, tallow leaf bright; TC, tallow canopy; TCMED, tallow canopy and leaf medium; TDRK, tallow leaf dark; TLF, tallow leaf; TMED, tallow leaf medium]

			Class stratified seeded			
Land class	Hyperion image swath and date	No. of training spectra from Hyperion image for PVA	Seeding with ground, canopy and created indicator spectra	PVA-output em	Analysis–Results	PVA indicator spectra used in spectral unmixing of Hyperion image (46 bands) to create percent occurrence maps
Hardwoods	ID -17 Oct 2009	8	Air_393, Air_384, Air_173, 2009_483, 2009_482 and			
			i) tallow leaf bright	none	no indicator for tallow discrimnation	
			ii) tallow leaf dark			
			iii) tallow leaf medium			
			iv) created tallow canopy and leaf medium(TCMED)			
Grasslands		9	Air_229, 2009_415M, 2009_410M, 2009_413, 2009_421	3em	may give a tallow indicator	no percent occurrence map of red trees
			Air_229, 2009_415M, 2009_410M, 2009_413, 2009_421 and	none	no indicator for tallow discrimnation	
			i) tallow leaf bright			
			ii) tallow leaf dark			
			iii) created tallow canopy and leaf medium(TCMED)			

Table 12.   PolyVector Analysis input database—helicopter and hyperion spectra.

[UTM15, Universal Transverse Mercator, zone 15; Air_*, fixed-wing plane survey field site]

Site names	Source	Site location
Heli-LiveVegetationwithChineseTallowtree	Helicopter	Seed-Indicator spectra
Heli-NonLiveVegetation	Helicopter	Seed-Indicator spectra
Heli-LiveVegetation	Helicopter	Seed-Indicator spectra
Hyp-ChineseTallowtreesinHardwoods-Airpoint1	Hyperion	Air_584
Hyp-ChineseTallowtreesinHardwoods-Airpoint2	Hyperion	Air_587
Hyp-RedtreesHardwoods-Airpoint3	Hyperion	Air_208
Hyp-RedtreesHardwoods-Airpoint4	Hyperion	Air_209
Hyp-RedGreenChineseTallowtreeedge-groundpoint5	Hyperion	2009_514
Hyp-ChineseTallowtreemoregreen-groundpoint6	Hyperion	2009_521
Hyp-GreenYellowChineseTallowtree-ground7	Hyperion	2009_480
Hyp-RowfenceChineseTallowtree-groundpoint8	Hyperion	2009_415M
Hyp-RedYellowGreenChineseTallowtree-groundpoint9	Hyperion	2009_505
Hyp-spectra1	Hyperion	434010E, 3510870N UTM15
Hyp-spectra2	Hyperion	432000E, 3503490N UTM15
Hyp-spectra3	Hyperion	440070E, 3503070N UTM15

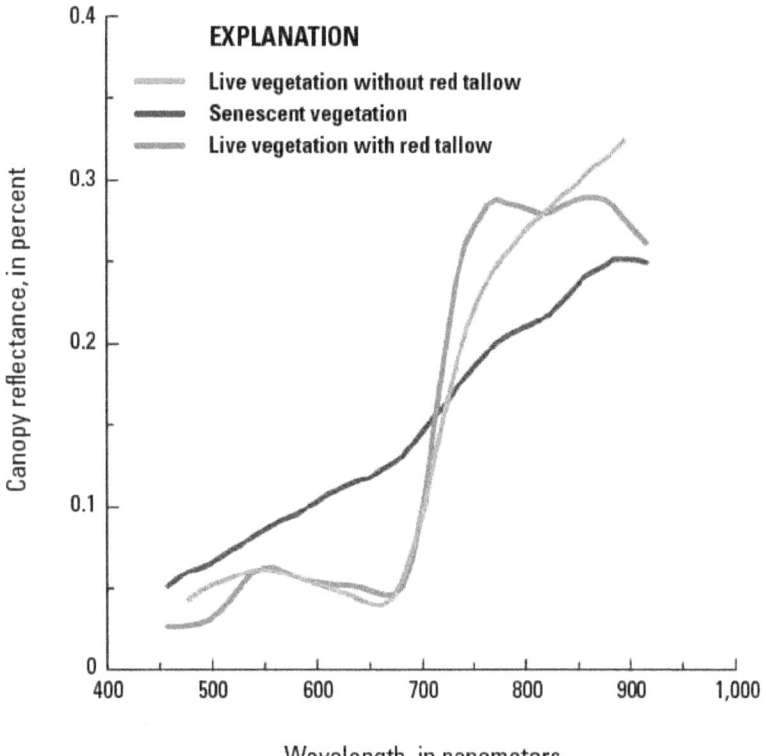

Figure 49.   Spectral indicators resulting from a PolyVector Analysis of helicopter-based (previously derived) indicator spectra and Hyperion-based spectra (table 13). Spectral indicators were sought for remotely sensed identification of red-leaf Chinese tallow tree (*Triadica sebifera*) within the Toledo Bend Reservoir study area (Louisiana and Texas).

Table 13. PolyVector Analysis output indicator spectra correlations. Correlations of the three indicator spectra representing helicopter-based live vegetation (with Chinese tallow tree [*Triadica sebifera*]) and non-live vegetation, seeded indicators, and hardwood with all input spectra extracted from the Hyperion reflectance image within the hardwood landcover. The entry in each cell provides the correlation magnitude between each spectra or location (row) in the input database and each indicator spectrum (column). The indicator spectra are identified by a column of ones and zeros.

[UTM15, Universal Transverse Mercator, zone 15; Air_*, fixed-wing plane survey field site. Red font signifies seed indicator spectrum, and green font denotes indicator spectra associated with ground and aerial sites]

Site names[1]	Site location	Indicator		
		1	2	3
LiveVegetationwithChineseTallowtree	Seed-Indicator Spectrum	0.0000	0.0000	1.0000
NonLiveVegetation	Seed-Indicator Spectrum	0.0000	1.0000	0.0000
LiveVegetation	Seed-Indicator Spectrum	0.0603	0.1719	0.7678
ChineseTallowtreeinHardwoods-Airpoint1	Air_584	0.9707	0.0503	-0.0210
ChineseTallowtreeinHardwoods-Airpoint2	Air_587	1.0000	0.0000	0.0000
RedtreesHardwoods-Airpoint3	Air_208	0.8612	0.1342	0.0046
RedtreesHardwoods-Airpoint4	Air_209	0.6967	0.2130	0.0903
RedGreenChineseTallowtreeedge-groundpoint5	2009_514	0.7194	0.2563	0.0243
ChineseTallowtreemoregreen-groundpoint6	2009_521	0.7644	0.2385	-0.0029
GreenYellowChineseTallowtree-groundpoint7	2009_480	0.7803	0.1478	0.0719
RowfenceChineseTallowtree-groundpoint8	2009_415M	0.6551	0.1610	0.1840
RedYellowGreenChineseTallowtree-groundpoint9	2009_505	0.5405	0.3709	0.0887
Hyperion Spectrum1	434010E, 3510870N UTM15	0.9044	0.1027	-0.0071
Hyperion Spectrum2	432000E, 3503490N UTM15	0.8297	0.1642	0.0061
Hyperion Spectrum3	440070E, 3503070N UTM15	0.9323	0.1288	-0.0611

[1]Seed-indicator spectra were created from helicopter recordings while the remaining spectra were extracted from the Hyperion reflectance image.

and spectra representing unknown (lacking ground or air observations) hardwood locations were near zero.

Results of the PVA processing of helicopter-based indicator spectra did not uniquely represent one canopy component, such as red-leaf Chinese tallow trees, but represented canopies likely or unlikely to contain some red-leaf Chinese tallow trees. The correlation magnitudes were related, but not necessarily directly related, to the percent occurrence of red trees or red-leaf Chinese tallow trees. The correlation magnitudes indicated greater or lesser degrees of similarity between the indicator spectrum and each spectrum in the input reflectance dataset (table 13) extracted from the Hyperion reflectance image. Correlation with Indicator 3 could simply represent similarity in overall spectrum shape, as reflected by the high correlation calculated with the other helicopter-based live vegetation spectra. The fact that this latter spectrum was associated with a location absent of Chinese tallow tree increased caution in direct interpretation of Chinese tallow tree or red tree occurrence predictions based on Indicator 3. Nevertheless, the preliminary validation based on ground and aerial observations provided a reasonable expectation that the set of three seed indicator spectra could provide mapped occurrences of the canopies most likely to contain some proportion of Chinese tallow trees or red trees. Based on that reasoning, the three indicator spectra were reformatted and entered into the PCI SPUNMIX procedure.

Subsequent applications of these PVA indicator spectra to the 1D swath Hyperion reflectance image by using the SPUNMIX procedure demonstrate a possibility that it could provide relative likelihoods of red-leaf Chinese tallow tree (or red tree) occurrences within senescing or live vegetation (figs. 50*A–C*). Limiting the occurrence mapping to the hardwood class and accounting for the misclassification associated with this land class (fig. 51), the predicted spatial distribution associated with each of the three indicator spectrum within the hardwood class were reasonable, particularly when associated with the live vegetation with Chinese tallow tree indicator spectrum. Although the likely occurrences of Chinese tallow trees or red trees, as represented by the live vegetation with Chinese tallow tree occurrence map, were spatially extensive, the associated magnitudes or percent occurrences associated with this spectral indicator were typically low (figs. 50 and 51).

Figure 50.   Maps representing percent occurrence of A, live vegetation, B, senescent vegetation, and C, live vegetation with red-leaf Chinese tallow trees (*Triadica sebifera*). The percent occurrence is represented by the grey intensity; a lighter grey reflects a higher percent occurrence, whereas a darker grey reflects a lower percent occurrence (or in this case likely occurrence) within the 30- by 30-meter Hyperion pixels. The coverages are within the Hyperion 1D swath.

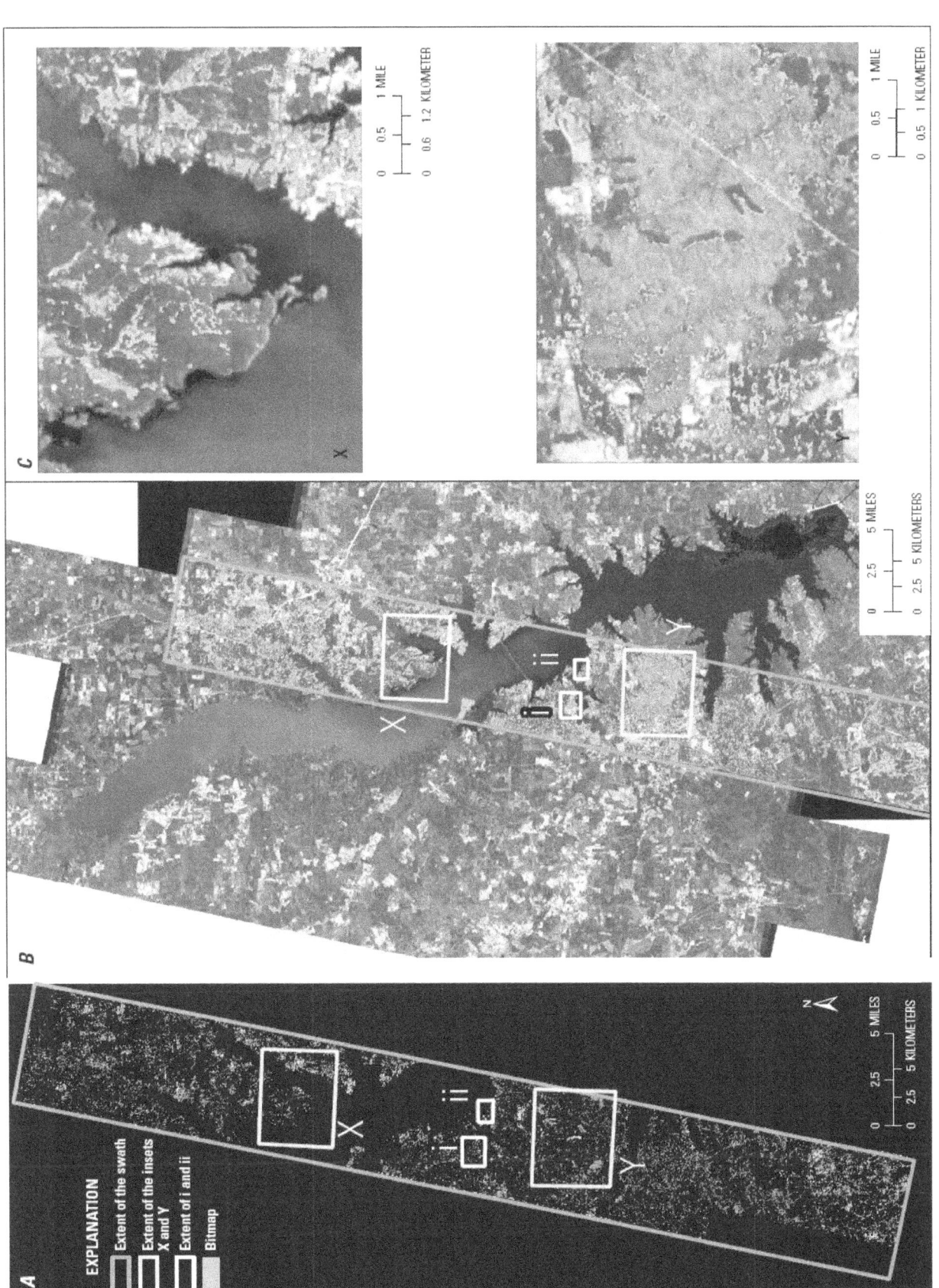

Figure 51.   Imagery showing the likelihood of Chinese tallow trees (*Triadica sebifera*) or red trees occurring within hardwood forest stands in the Toledo Bend Reservoir study area (Louisiana and Texas). *A*, Map showing percent predicted likelihood of Chinese tallow trees or red trees occurring within hardwood stands (recreated from fig. 50*C*). *B*, The binomial representation of *A* with yellow highlighting of pixels in the Hyperion image (1D swath) to indicate all areas with a likelihood greater than zero of Chinese tallow tree or red tree occurrences within hardwood stands (binomial mask is overlain on the Advanced Land Imager [ALI] false-color image). *C*, Insets "X" and "Y" illuminate areas of predicted occurrences with ground-based observations. Insets "i" and "ii" recreated in figure 52 illustrate the association of predicted occurrences as depicted on the ALI image.

As illustrated on the insets (fig. 51C X), likely occurrences of vegetation containing red Chinese tallow tree are associated with senescing hardwood-bottomland stands. As observed in the fixed-wing survey, actual occurrences were fewer than exhibited in the percent occurrence map. The overestimation is related in part to occurrences associated with non-hardwood classes that had been misidentified as hardwoods in the ALI classification. In contrast, on the opposite shore (fig. 51C Y), relatively few likely occurrences of red-leaf Chinese tallow tree are contained in the large hardwood stand in the southwestern portion of the Hyperion 1D swath. In addition, ground observations (photographs corresponding to fig. 52 i) tend to support the association of the predicted likelihoods of the hardwood containing red-leaf Chinese tallow tree or red trees as observed at the location captured in the aerial photograph corresponding to figure 52 ii. Overall, the predictions of red tree or red-leaf Chinese tallow tree occurrences were promising. Even though promising, they seemed more related to the likelihood of live vegetation containing some percentage of red tree or red-leaf Chinese tallow tree. In that context, the procedure performed as expected.

The limitation of the product was in the inability to directly validate the prediction accuracy or to directly apply this information to detecting red-leaf Chinese tallow trees. Based on the PVA association results (table 13) and the occurrence distribution (fig. 51A and C inset Y and fig. 52 ii), the spectral indicator seemed to discriminate between senescing hardwood stands likely to contain red-leaf Chinese tallow trees and senescing hardwoods stands not likely to contain red-leaf Chinese tallow trees. Selection was not broadcast over all senescing hardwoods but only certain hardwood stands. The implication was that the predicted percent-occurrence magnitudes were related to an increased likelihood of red tree or red-leaf Chinese tallow tree occurrence; however, the accuracy of such likelihood predictions could not be determined based on ancillary or collected information. Nevertheless, because supporting evidence bolstered those likelihood predictions, this analysis and mapping method was applied to the other landcover classes and multiple Hyperion swath coverages.

Extending PolyVector Analysis (PVA) Mapping with Helicopter-Based Indicator Spectra to Multiple Landcover Clases and Hyperion Swaths

In the extended mapping analyses, spectral databases were produced for all the major classes identified in the ALI classification: hardwoods, grasslands, planted pine, and mature pine; each of the priority Hyperion swaths (1D, 2C, 6E, 7B, and 4F); and for up to three dates for each swath-landcover class. An independent PVA input database was constructed for each variation in landcover class, swath, and date, and for each of these combinations, two different seed indicator sets were applied: one containing and one without a red-leaf Chinese tallow tree reflectance spectra. The format of each constructed input database and the PVA or SPUNMIX operational procedures followed the hardwood landcover class 1D swath example as described in the "Seeding with Helicopter-Based Indicator Spectra" section. Although confining each input database by land class decreased the variance input into PVA, it multiplied the number of databases that had to be constructed. Results of these applications are summarized and reported in table 14 and in the interactive version of that table available from the Web index page of this report.

Landcover is the top-level division in table 14. Landcover is subdivided into Hyperion swaths (see fig. 11), and each swath is subdivided subsequently by collection date. Each collection date is associated with a hotlink to a datasheet containing the spectral database input into the PVA. Clicking on the hotlink retrieves the actual input datasheet used. PVA was applied to each input datasheet after including seed indicator spectra. Two indicator spectra sets were entered. The first contained only the "Helicopter-Vegetation with Tallow" and the "Nonlive Material" spectra (see fig. 45). The second additionally contained the "Known Red Tallow Leaf" spectrum (see fig. 26). The last column contains hotlinks to datasheets containing the PVA results based on the two indicator spectra sets (with and without the "Known Red Tallow" spectrum). In the PVA results datasheets, the seed indicator spectra correlations are highlighted in grey and indicator spectra associated with nonseed indicator spectra are highlighted in brown. Next, the PVA output indicator spectra correlations (results listed in the last column of table 14) were then used in the SPUNMIX spectral unmixing algorithm.

The transformation of Hyperion image data to percent-occurrence image per landcover class did not consistently correspond with the observed and possible Chinese tallow tree occurrences as recorded during ground and aerial surveys. The predicted percent-occurrence maps did not show any consistent pattern per swath, date, or land cover class that could be associated with likely occurrence of Chinese tallow trees (or red trees).

Discussion and Conclusion

Unprecedented and coordinated field and EO-1 NASA Hyperion and ALI data collections of the Toledo Bend Reservoir area were carried out between 2009 and early 2011. In total, 24 clear-sky Hyperion and ALI image pairs were collected and 801 field ground and aerial field points were documented during the fall to early winter seasons of Chinese tallow tree senescence. The coordinated collections emphasized detection of senescing red-leaf Chinese tallow tree by linking observed occurrences to changes in the Hyperion data transformed to canopy reflectance. Linkage was performed by deriving Chinese tallow tree indicator spectra from the Hyperion canopy reflectance, helicopter-based canopy reflectance, and leaf-reflectance datasets. Segmentation by an ALI-based landcover class enhanced the subpixel detection performance.

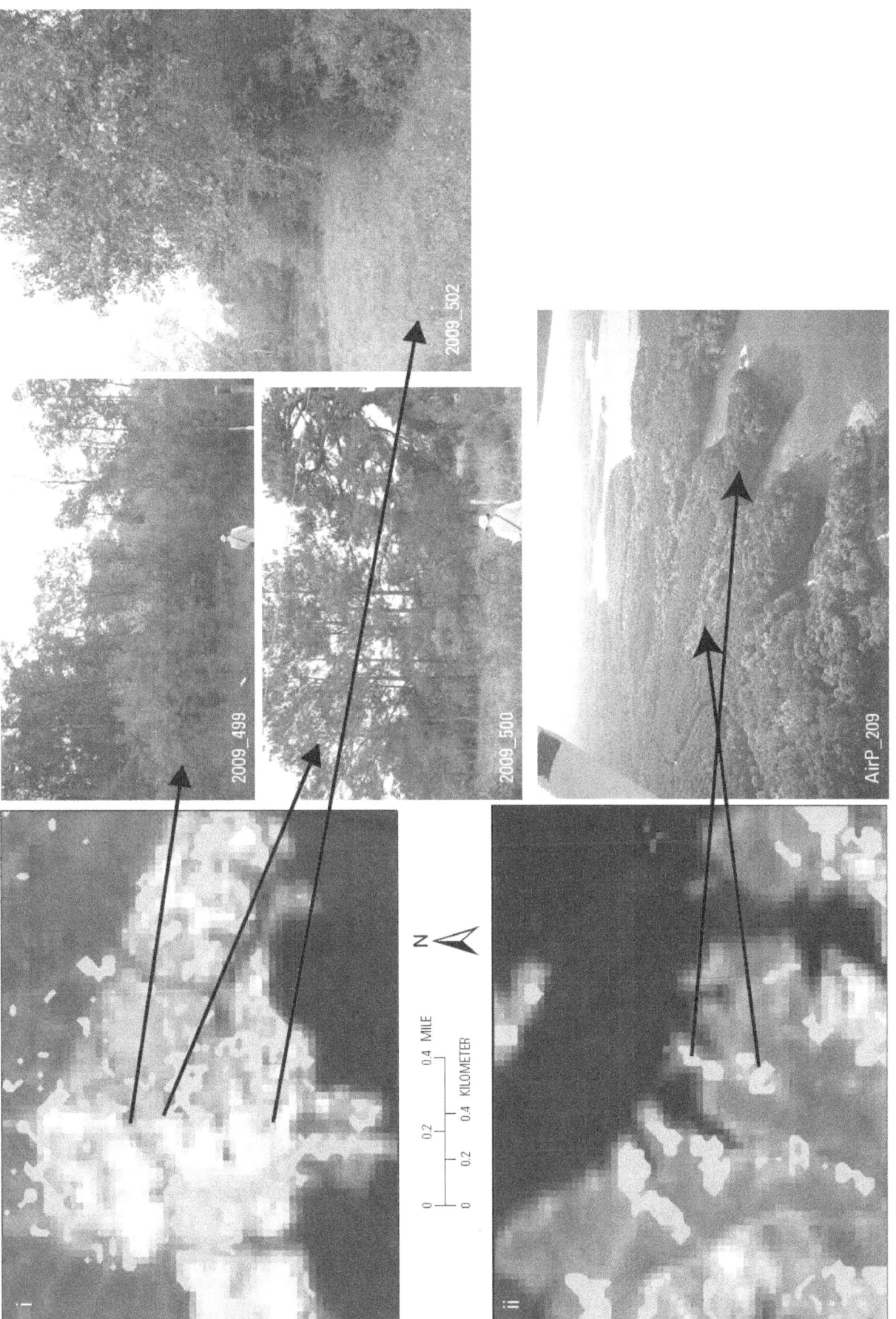

Figure 52. Illustrations detailing possible associations between spectrally indicated predictions of likely occurrences of red-leaf Chinese tallow trees (*Triadica sebifera*) and observed occurrences documented (by photography) during aerial and ground reconnaissance within the Toledo Bend Reservoir study area (Louisiana and Texas). The area corresponding to inset i of figure 51B is labeled "i," and the area corresponding to inset ii of figure 51B is labeled "ii." The names on the photographs, for example 2009_499, indicate the site names.

Table 14.   Mapping vegetation likely associated with red-leaf Chinese tallow tree (*Triadica sebifera*) occurrences.

| Land class | Hyperion image | | Number of input Hyperion reflec- tance spectra | Seeding with Indicator spectra | | | PolyVector Analysis output -indicator spec- tra correlations |
	Swath	Date		Helicopter- veg- etation with Chinese tal- low tree	Non-live material	Known red tallow leaf	
Hardwoods	1D	11-Nov-09	23	X	X		Results-1
				X	X	X	Results-2
		20-Dec-09	16	X	X		Results-1
				X	X	X	Results-2
		5-Nov-10	17	X	X		Results-1
				X	X	X	Results-2
	2C	4-Nov-09	25	X	X		Results-1
				X	X	X	Results-2
		1-Dec-10	25	X	X		Results-1
				X	X	X	Results-2
	6E	25-Dec-09	22	X	X		Results-1
				X	X	X	Results-2
		24-Dec-10	16	X	X		Results-1
				X	X	X	Results-2
	7B	19-Dec-10	25	X	X		Results-1
				X	X	X	Results-2
	4F	18-Oct-10	8	X	X		Results-1
				X	X	X	Results-2
Grasslands	1D	11-Nov-09	12	X	X		Results-1
				X	X	X	Results-2
		20-Dec-09	23	X	X		Results-1
				X	X	X	Results-2
		5-Nov-10	23	X	X		Results-1
				X	X	X	Results-2
	2C	4-Nov-09	12	X	X		Results-1
				X	X	X	Results-2
		1-Dec-10	11	X	X		Results-1
				X	X	X	Results-2
	6E	25-Dec-09	16	X	X		Results-1
				X	X	X	Results-2
		24-Dec-10	6	X	X		Results-1
				X	X	X	Results-2
	7B	19-Dec-10	11	X	X		Results-1
				X	X	X	Results-2
	4F	18-Oct-10	5	X	X		Results-1
				X	X	X	Results-2
Planted Pine	1D	11-Nov-09	16	X	X		Results-1
				X	X	X	Results-2
		20-Dec-09	14	X	X		Results-1
				X	X	X	Results-2
		5-Nov-10	14	X	X		Results-1
				X	X	X	Results-2

Table 14. Mapping vegetation likely associated with red-leaf Chinese tallow tree (*Triadica sebifera*) occurrences.—Continued

| Land class | Hyperion image | | Number of input Hyperion reflectance spectra | Seeding with Indicator spectra | | | PolyVector Analysis output -indicator spectra correlations |
	Swath	Date		Helicopter- vegetation with Chinese tallow tree	Non-live material	Known red tallow leaf	
	2C	4-Nov-09	19	X	X		Results-1
				X	X	X	Results-2
		1-Dec-10	19	X	X		Results-1
				X	X	X	Results-2
	6E	25-Dec-09	15	X	X		Results-1
				X	X	X	Results-2
		24-Dec-10	10	X	X		Results-1
				X	X	X	Results-2
	7B	19-Dec-10	13	X	X		Results-1
				X	X	X	Results-2
	4F	18-Oct-10	13	X	X		Results-1
				X	X	X	Results-2
Mature Pine	1D	11-Nov-09	13	X	X		Results-1
				X	X	X	Results-2
		20-Dec-09	13	X	X		Results-1
				X	X	X	Results-2
		5-Nov-10	13	X	X		Results-1
				X	X	X	Results-2
	2C	4-Nov-09	18	X	X		Results-1
				X	X	X	Results-2
		1-Dec-10	18	X	X		Results-1
				X	X	X	Results-2
	6E	25-Dec-09	14	X	X		Results-1
				X	X	X	Results-2
		24-Dec-10	10	X	X		Results-1
				X	X	X	Results-2
	7B	19-Dec-10	12	X	X		Results-1
				X	X	X	Results-2
	4F	18-Oct-10	4	X	X		Results-1
				X	X	X	Results-2

Field Reconnaissance

Field reconnaissance provided critical information about the distribution of Chinese tallow tree and located sites of known occurrences that were used to calibrate and validate the performance of the detection process. Ground and aerial surveys suggest that Chinese tallow tree occurrences are infrequent and scattered without any observed pattern relative to the Toledo Bend Reservoir. The only pattern that did exist was the sporadic but repetitive occurrence of Chinese tallow tree along forest edges, water edges, and fence lines, probably most in line with seed dispersal by birds. Even though densities were low, Chinese tallow trees were observed to be more densely dispersed within some scrublands and grasslands than within pine, hardwood, and mixed forests. Excluding a couple of seemingly nonmanaged planted pine fields, we did not observe any notable establishment of Chinese tallow trees in the ubiquitous pine plantations. If the understory red trees observed in the hardwood fingers are Chinese tallow trees, the highest potential threat from this invasive species is most likely related to the close spatial association of pine plantations and hardwood fingers.

Problems in identifying Chinese tallow tree in aerial, and even on the ground surveys in 2009 and, especially, in 2010, were the high proportion of the foliage was green instead of red. Another problem in detection was related to spectral confusion. Spectral analyses of tree leaves collected throughout the study area found that red maple and sweetgum trees could contain senescing red leaves that were spectrally similar to Chinese tallow tree senescing red leaves. That confusion caused ambiguity in the identification of red-leafed trees as Chinese tallow trees in the aerial surveys. In order to acknowledge that identification confusion, the term "red trees" was applied to all observations of red-leafed trees during aerial surveys.

Chinese tallow tree, or for that matter red maple and sweetgum trees containing senescing red leaves, were uncommon at the top of canopy (TOC) position within mature pine or hardwood canopies and within pine plantations, scrublands, and grassland fields. Unless these understory red trees were observable through gaps in the canopy, it was unlikely they could be detected in the canopy-reflectance spectra whether derived from aerial or the Hyperion image data. Furthermore, where red-leaf Chinese tallow trees did occur, the percent occurrences within multiple and contiguous 30- by 30-m patches (size of area determined to simulate the Hyperion IFOV as represented as image pixels) were extremely low. The highest frequency of observed concentrations of red-leaf Chinese tallow trees and red trees were found in isolated small patches containing scattered shrubs or one to two canopy trees (figs. 24 (HS15), 33A, and 35E–H). As an estimate, the two TOC-positioned red-leaf Chinese tallow trees (figs. 38A and B) could encompass an area of 9–36 m^2 that, if perfectly contained in a single 30-m^2 patch, would account for a 1–4 percent occurrence in the Hyperion pixel.

Creation of Workable Calibration Spectra

Previous work discussed in the "Background" section found that 10 percent occurrence rates of red-leaf Chinese tallow trees were accurately detected in a Hyperion pixel 68 percent of the time and 15 percent Chinese tallow trees 85 percent of the time (fig. 5; Ramsey and others, 2005b). Three to four TOC-positioned mature Chinese tallow trees fully foliated with red leaves could represent upwards of 10 percent coverage within a single Hyperion pixel. Similarly, tens of Chinese tallow tree shrubs fully foliated with red leaves in an open area could comprise 10 percent of a pixel. As confirmed in the same studies, however, red-leaf Chinese tallow trees making up much less than 10 percent of the Hyperion pixel were often detected. Although the detection accuracy at a 10 percent occurrence threshold is 68 percent, detection of red-leaf Chinese tallow tree at lower percentages of occurrence was not excluded. The accuracy of detection at increasingly lower occurrence rates became progressively lower.

In this project, few observed occurrences of red-leaf Chinese tallow trees reached 1 to 4 percent coverage within the 30- by 30-m Hyperion pixel. Given the detection-accuracy threshold of 68 percent associated with vegetation coverage of 10 percent of the pixel (much higher than what we observed), it was unknown whether or not we could identify a workable set of calibration spectra from the canopy reflectance data. For Ramsey and others (2005b), we had created a successful detection-calibration spectrum for red-leaf Chinese tallow trees by using canopy-reflection spectra extracted from Hyperion reflectance images. For that study, we had used helicopter-based spectra to cross-validate the set of spectra derived from the Hyperion images. In effect, procedures in the current study largely followed those previously successful methods, with the most important difference being the lack of red-leaf Chinese tallow trees occurring at or above 10 percent coverage within the Toledo Bend Reservoir study area.

Attempting the Detection of Chinese Tallow Tree with Calibration Spectra

Even though the scarcity of Chinese tallow trees caused a challenge in building a workable spectral calibration dataset for Hyperion subpixel detection, calibration datasets were constructed. The initial calibration datasets included canopy-reflectance spectra of selected locations where ground and aerial reconnaissance provided known presence or absence of red-leaf Chinese tallow trees (or red trees) and of locations where presence or absence of Chinese tallow tree occurrences were unknown were extracted from Hyperion reflectance images. In these initial attempts to identify calibration spectra, all land classes were combined within a single dataset, but this procedure failed to identify a set of calibration spectra capable of distinctly identifying the targeted vegetation. The failure of the first procedure led to separating the Hyperion reflectance datasets by landcover classes (based on the ALI classification map). Separating the data by class tended to reduce the variance of the input dataset, thereby promoting spectral discrimination and raising the performance of the spectral analysis. Added to these class-based reflectance calibration datasets were spectra with known associations with red-leaf Chinese tallow trees. These known spectra included results of previous Chinese tallow tree mapping projects (Ramsey and others, 2005b), leaf spectra collected during the current study, and modified spectra from the canopy and leaf data. The addition of these seed spectra was intended to guide the program used to identify the calibration spectra. Unfortunately, none of these attempts resulted in an unambiguous set of calibration spectra with reliable capability to detect red-leaf Chinese tallow tree occurrences within the Toledo Bend Reservoir study area (table 14). The scarcity of red-leaf Chinese tallow tree occurrences in the study area prevented identifying a set of calibration spectra that would specifically detect it.

Even though specificity in detecting Chinese tallow tree was lacking, based on indirect evidence, primarily aerial photography that spatially coincided with predicted occurrences, a pattern emerged that indicated the more spatially expansive predicted distributions were more likely to incorporate observed locations of red-leaf Chinese tallow tree than not. The associated pattern, however, changed from one produced map to the next. No one set of spectral indicators produced more consistent results or clear patterns of association than did another. Although the likely association was tenuous, we examined the helicopter-based spectral indicator set with the idea in mind of mapping vegetation associations within a class that had higher likelihoods of containing red-leaf Chinese tallow trees, instead of directly detecting and mapping specific occurrences.

Indicator Spectra Derived from Helicopter-Based Reflectance Spectra

The helicopter-based spectral indicator set was chosen because it offered a single indicator set and was directly identified from canopy-reflectance spectra representing observed red-leaf Chinese tallow tree occurrences and vegetation classes. The drawbacks were related to the limited number of landcover classes represented, inherent noise, and lack of a specific Chinese tallow tree indicator spectrum. Even with these drawbacks, we believed the canopy spectra derived from helicopter and simultaneous ground measurements provided the best opportunity to construct likelihood of occurrence maps that could be interpreted with respect to red-leaf Chinese tallow trees.

The helicopter-based spectral indicator set was integrated into spectral calibration datasets representing each major landcover class in each of the five Hyperion swaths that make up the priority coverage of the dominant landcover classes in the study area. Predicted occurrences produced from these calibration datasets illustrated a possibility of creating occurrence maps that would indicate vegetation associations most likely to contain Chinese tallow trees, instead of specific

occurrences of the species itself. Inspection of output datasets showed mixed performance in the differential alignment of each indicator spectrum with vegetations likely or unlikely to contain red-leaf Chinese tallow trees (or red trees). Similarly, predicted occurrence maps exhibited no overall consistent pattern per landcover class or per Hyperion swath that could be solely associated with likely Chinese tallow tree occurrences. At times, the predicted distribution appeared promising; however, at many other times the predicted distribution of red-leaf Chinese tallow trees (or red trees) co-occurred with nearly the entire land class distribution. Ultimately, the inability to fully evaluate the predicted relationship of Chinese tallow trees with particular vegetation associations within each land class prevented further analyses of this possible relationship.

Implications for Future Mapping Efforts

As observed in the ground and aerial surveys, even though Chinese tallow tree occurrences are scattered and its numbers are low, the distribution is widespread throughout the study area. These scattered occurrences, combined with landscape dynamics and the bird-dispersal mechanism, indicate the potential for further spread in the study area unless contained by natural forces or management strategies. Future efforts to document and control the spread of this invasive species in the Toledo Bend Reservoir area can benefit from the current study. We suggest that a high spectral resolution sensor similar to the Hyperion but with an increased signal-to-noise level and, most importantly, a higher ground-level spatial resolution would better detect Chinese tallow tree at the present level of occurrences. A 10- by 10-m ground-level spatial resolution would increase the detectable range of Chinese tallow tree occurrences from less than 5 percent to 45 percent of the ground pixel, which would be well above the maximum range associated with the successful mapping of the species in southwestern Louisiana. Aircraft and sensor systems are available to conduct high spectral mapping at this ground-level spatial resolution and much higher. Built on the knowledge and baseline databases and maps developed in this study, the probable success rate of mapping with a higher ground-level spatial resolution and a higher spectral resolution is high.

References Cited

DeLoach, C.J. and J.L. Tracy. 1997. Effects of Biological Control of Saltcedar (*Tamarix ramosissima*) on Endangered Species: Biological Assessment, 17 October 1997. USDA/ARS, Temple, TX, 612 pg.

Ehrlich, Robert., 2000, The PVA multivariate unmixing system, self-training classification (Salt Lake City, UT: Tramontane, Inc. and C&E Enterprises).

Howard, Mark, 2009. GIS Administrator, Sabine River Authority of Texas, Personal Communication.

PCI Geomatics, 2005, Using Geomatica 10, Richmond Hill, Ontario, Canada, PCI Geomatics.

Ramsey III, Elijah, and Jensen, John, 1995, Modelling mangrove canopy reflectance using a light interaction model and an optimization technique, *in* Lyon, J.G., and McCarthy, Jack, Wetland and environmental applications of GIS: Boca Raton, Fla., CRC Press, Inc., p. 61–81.

Ramsey III, Elijah, and Laine, Steve, 1997, Comparison of Landsat Thematic Mapper and high resolution photography to identify change in complex coastal marshes: Journal of Coastal Research, v. 13, no. 2, 281–292.

Ramsey III, Elijah, and Nelson, Gene, 2005, A whole image approach for transforming EO1 Hyperion hyperspectral data into highly accurate reflectance data with site-specific measurements: International Journal of Remote Sensing, v. 26, no. 8, 1589–1610.

Ramsey III, Elijah, Nelson, Gene, and Sapkota, Sijan, 2001, Coastal change analysis program implemented in Louisiana: Journal of Coastal Research, v. 17, no. 1, 55–71.

Ramsey III, Elijah, Nelson, Gene, Sapkota, Sijan, Seeger, Eric, and Martella, Kristine, 2002, Mapping Chinese Tallow with color-infrared photography: Photogrammetric Engineering and Remote Sensing, v. 68, no. 3, 251–255.

Ramsey III, Elijah, Rangoonwala, Amina, Nelson, Gene, and Ehrlich, Robert, 2005a, Mapping the invasive species, Chinese Tallow, with EO1 satellite Hyperion hyperspectral image data and relating tallow percent occurrences to a classified Landsat Thematic Mapper landcover map: International Journal of Remote Sensing, v. 26, no. 8, 1637–1657.

Ramsey III, Elijah, Rangoonwala, Amina, Nelson, Gene, Ehrlich, Robert, and Martella, Kristine, 2005b, Generation and validation of characteristic spectra from EO1 Hyperion image data for detecting the percent occurrence of invasive species, specifically Chinese Tallow: International Journal of Remote Sensing, v. 26, no. 8, 1611–1636.

Richter R., and Schläpfer, D., 2011, Atmospheric / Topographic Correction for Satellite Imagery, DLR report DLR-IB 565-02/11, Wessling, Germany, pp 202.

The Nature Conservancy, 1998, the dirty dozen—America's least wanted: The Nature Conservancy, Conservation Science Bulletin (http://plants.usda.gov/plantguide/pdf/pg_trse6.pdf).

U.S. Department of Agriculture, 2011, PLANTS Database: U.S. Department of Agriculture, Natural Resources Conservation Service, accessed October 21, 2011, at http://plants.usda.gov/java/.

Westbooks, Randy, 1998, Invasive plants, changing the landscape of America—Fact book: Washington, D.C., Federal Interagency Committee for the Management of Noxious and Exotic Weeds, 109 p.

Publishing support provided by
Lafayette Publishing Service Center

Ramsey and others—Remote Sensing Survey of Chinese Tallow Tree in the Toledo Bend Reservoir Area, Louisiana and Texas—Open-File Report 2012-1215